Simply Shakespeare

Original Shakespearean Text
With a Modern Line-for-Line Translation

MACBETH

BARRON'S

All inquiries should be addressed to:
Barron's Educational Series, Inc.
250 Wireless Boulevard
Hauppauge, New York 11788
http://www.barronseduc.com

ISBN-13: 978-0-7641-2086-2
ISBN-10: 0-7641-2086-7

Library of Congress Catalog Card No. 2001043294

Library of Congress Cataloging-in-Publication Data

Shakespeare, William, 1564–1616.
    Macbeth / edited and rendered into modern English by Robert R. Roth.
        p. cm. — (Simply Shakespeare)
    Includes bibliographical references.
    Summary: Presents the original text of Shakespeare's play side by side with a modern version, with discussion questions, role-playing scenarios, and other study activities.
    ISBN 0-7641-2086-7
        1. Macbeth, King of Scotland, 11th cent.—Juvenile drama. 2. Regicides—Juvenile drama. 3. Scotland—Juvenile drama. 4. Children's plays, English. [1. Shakespeare, William, 1564–1616. Macbeth. 2. Plays. 3. English literature—History and criticism.] I. Roth, Robert R., 1949– II. Title.

PR2823 .A25 2002
822.3'3—dc21

                                      2001043294

PRINTED IN CHINA
30 29 28 27 26 25

Simply Shakespeare

Titles in the Series

Contents

Introduction

William Shakespeare, 1564–1616

Who was William Shakespeare? This simple question has challenged scholars for years. The man behind vivid, unforgettable characters like Hamlet, Romeo and Juliet, and King Lear is a shadow compared to his creations. Luckily, official records of Shakespeare's time have preserved some facts about his life.

Shakespeare was born in April 1564 in Stratford-upon-Avon, England. His father, John Shakespeare, was a prominent local merchant. Shakespeare probably attended grammar school in Stratford, learning basic Latin and Greek and studying works by ancient Roman writers. In 1582, when Shakespeare was 18, he married Anne Hathaway. Eventually, the couple had three children—but, like many families in their day, they were forced to endure a tragic loss when Hamnet, their only son, died at age 11.

No records document Shakespeare's life from 1585 to 1592, when he was between the ages of 21 and 28. In his writings, Shakespeare seems to know so much about so many things that it's tempting to make guesses about how he supported his young family during this period. Over the years, it's been speculated that he worked as a schoolteacher, a butcher, or an actor—and even that he did a little poaching as a young man. Thanks to some London theater gossip left behind by a professional rival, we know that Shakespeare was living in London as a playwright and an actor by 1592. Meanwhile, Anne and the children stayed in Stratford.

This must have been a thrilling time for Shakespeare. In 1592, England was becoming a powerful nation under its great and clever queen, Elizabeth I. English explorers and colonists crossed seas to search strange new worlds. London was a bustling, exciting center of commerce, full of travelers from abroad. And though many Europeans still looked down on English culture, they admitted that London's stages boasted some of the best plays and actors to be found. Travelers from all over admired the dramas of Christopher Marlowe, Thomas Kyd, and the new name on the scene, William Shakespeare.

Nevertheless, the life of the theater had its hazards. London's actors, playwrights, and theatrical entrepreneurs chose a risky and somewhat shady line of work. Religious leaders condemned the theater for encouraging immorality and idleness among the London populace. London's city leaders, fearful of crowds, closed the theaters in times of unrest or plague. Luckily, the London troupes had some powerful "fans"—members of the nobility who acted as patrons, protecting the troupes from their enemies. Queen Elizabeth herself loved plays. Special performances were regularly given for her at court.

By 1594, two theatrical companies had emerged as the most popular. Archrivals, The Lord Admiral's Men and The Lord Chamberlain's Men performed at the Rose and the Theatre, respectively. However, The Lord Chamberlain's Men had an ace: Shakespeare was both a founding member and the company's main playwright. The company's fine lead actor was Richard Burbage, the first man to play such roles as Hamlet, Othello, and Macbeth. With a one-two punch like that, it's not surprising that The Lord Chamberlain's Men soon emerged as London's top troupe. By 1597, Shakespeare had written such works as *Romeo and Juliet, The Merchant of Venice,* and *A Midsummer Night's Dream.* His finances grew with his reputation, and he was able to buy land and Stratford's second-largest house, where Anne and the children moved while he remained in London.

Then as now, owning property went a long way. Like many acting companies to this day, The Lord Chamberlain's Men got involved in a bitter dispute with their landlord. However, they owned the actual timbers of the Theatre building—which turned out to be useful assets. Eventually the exasperated troupe hired a builder to secretly take apart the Theatre, then transported its timbers across London to the south bank of the River Thames. There, they used the Theatre's remains to construct their new home—The Globe.

At The Globe, many of Shakespeare's greatest plays first came to life. From 1599 until his death in 1616, the open-air Globe served as Shakespeare's main stage. Audiences saw the first performances of *Hamlet, Macbeth, Twelfth Night,* and *King Lear* there. (In winter, Shakespeare's company performed at London's Blackfriars, the indoor theater that housed the first performance of *The Tempest.*) In 1603, after the death of Queen Elizabeth, Shakespeare's troupe added a new triumph to its résumé. Changing its name to The King's Men, it became the official theatrical company of England's new monarch, James I. The company performed frequently at court and state functions for its powerful new patron.

Around 1611–1612, Shakespeare returned permanently to Stratford. Unfortunately, we know little about his domestic life there. Where Shakespeare is concerned, there's no "tell-all" biography to reveal his intimate life. Was he happily wed to Anne, or did he live for so long in London to escape a bad marriage? Do the sonnets Shakespeare published in 1609 tell us a real-life story of his relationships with a young man, a "Dark Lady," and a rival for the lady's love? What were Shakespeare's political beliefs? From his writings, it's clear that Shakespeare understood life's best and worst emotions very deeply. But we'll never know how much of his own life made its way into his art. He died at the age of 53 on April 23, 1616, leaving behind the almost 40 plays and scores of poems that have spoken for him to generations of readers and listeners. Shakespeare is buried in Holy Trinity Church in Stratford, where he lies under a stone that warns the living—in verse—never to disturb his bones.

Shakespeare's Theater

Going to a play in Shakespeare's time was a completely different experience than going to a play today. How theaters were built, who attended, what happened during the performance, and who produced the plays were all quite unlike most theater performances today.

Theaters in Shakespeare's time were mainly outside the walls of the city of London—and away from the authorities *in* London. In those times, many religious authorities (especially radical Protestants) condemned plays and playgoing. They preached that plays, being stage illusions, were acts of deception and therefore sinful. The city authorities in London agreed that the theaters encouraged immorality. Despite this, theaters did exist in and around the city of London. They were, however, housed in neighborhoods known as Liberties. Liberties were areas that previously had religious functions and therefore were under the control of the crown, not the city of London. Luckily for playgoers, the monarchs Elizabeth and James were more tolerant of the amusements offered by the stage than the London authorities.

Who enjoyed what the stage had to offer? Almost all of London society went to the theater. Merchants and their wives, prostitutes, lawyers, laborers, and visitors from other countries would attend. Once you were at the theater, your social station dictated what you could pay and where you sat. If you could only afford a pence (about a penny), you would stand in the yard immediately surrounding the stage.

(These members of Shakespeare's audience were called "groundlings.") As many as a thousand other spectators might join you there. In the yard everyone would be exposed to the weather and to peddlers selling fruit and nuts. Your experience would probably be more active and less quiet than attending a play today. Movement was not uncommon. If you wanted a better or different view, you might rove about the yard. If you paid another pence, you could move into a lower gallery.

The galleries above and surrounding the stage on all sides could accommodate up to 2,000 more people. However, because the galleries were vertical and surrounded the stage, no matter where you sat, you would never be more than 35 feet away from the stage. The galleries immediately behind the stage were reserved for members of the nobility and royalty. From behind the stage a noble could not only see everything, but—more importantly—could be seen by others in the audience! Queen Elizabeth and King James were less likely to attend a theater performance, although they protected theater companies. Instead, companies performed plays for them at court.

The Globe's stage was similar to the other outdoor theaters in Shakespeare's time. These stages offered little decoration or frills. Consequently, the actors and the text carried the burden of delivering the drama. Without the help of scenery or lighting, the audience had to imagine what was not represented on the stage (the storms, shipwrecks, and so forth). The Globe's stage was rectangular—with dimensions of about 27 by 44 feet. At the back of the stage was a curtained wall containing three entrances onto the stage. These entrances led directly from the tiring (as in "attiring") house, where the actors would dress. The middle entrance was covered by a hanging tapestry and was probably used for special entrances—such as a ceremonial procession or the delivery of a prologue.

Unlike the yard, the stage was covered by a canopied roof that was suspended by two columns. This canopy was known as the *heavens.* Its underside was covered with paintings of the sun, moon, stars, and sky and was visible to all theatergoers. *Hell* was the area below the stage with a trapdoor as the entrance. Immediately behind and one flight above the stage were the dressing rooms, and above them lay the storage area for props and costumes.

Indoor theaters were similar to outdoor theaters in many respects. They featured a bare stage with the heavens, a trapdoor leading to hell, and doors leading to the tiring house. Builders created indoor theaters from preexisting space in already constructed buildings. These theaters were smaller, and because they were in town they were also more expensive. Standing in the yard of an outdoor theater cost a pence. The cheapest seat in an *indoor* theater was sixpence. The most fashionable and wealthy members of London society attended indoor theaters as much to see as to be seen. If you were a gallant (a fashionable theater-goer), you could pay 24 pence and actually sit on a stool at the edge of the stage—where everyone could see you.

The actors' costumes were also on display. Whether plays were performed indoors or outdoors, costumes were richly decorated. They were one of the main assets of a theater company and one of the draws of theater. However, costumes didn't necessarily match the period of the play's setting. How spectacular the costumes looked was more important than how realistic they were or if they matched the period setting.

These costumes were worn on stage only by men or boys who were a part of licensed theater companies. The actors in the companies were exclusively male and frequently doubled up on parts. Boys played female roles before their voices changed. Some actors were also shareholders—the most important members of a theater company. The shareholders owned the company's assets (the play texts, costumes, and props) and made a profit from the admissions gathered. Besides the shareholders and those actors who did not hold shares, other company members were apprentices and hired men and musicians.

The actors in Shakespeare's day worked hard. They were paid according to the house's take. New plays were staged rapidly, possibly with as little as three weeks from the time a company first received the play text until opening night. All the while, the companies appeared to have juggled a large number of new and older plays in performance. In lead roles, the most popular actors might have delivered as many as 4,000 lines in six different plays during a London working week! Working at this pace, it seems likely that teamwork was key to a company's success.

The Sound of Shakespeare

Shakespeare's heroes and heroines all share one quality: They're all great talkers. They combine Shakespeare's powerful imagery and vocabulary with a sound that thunders, trills, rocks, and sings.

When Shakespearean actors say their lines, they don't just speak lines of dialogue. Often, they're also speaking lines of dramatic poetry that are written in a sound pattern called *iambic pentameter.* When these lines don't rhyme and are not grouped in stanzas, they're called *blank verse*. Though many passages in Shakespeare plays are written in prose, the most important and serious moments are almost always in iambic pentameter. As Shakespeare matured, the sound of his lines began to change. Late plays like *The Tempest* are primarily in a wonderfully flowing blank verse. Earlier works, such as *Romeo and Juliet,* feature much more rhymed iambic pentameter, often with punctuation at the end of each line to make the rhymes even stronger.

Terms like "iambic pentameter" sound scarily technical—like part of a chemistry experiment that will blow up the building if you measure it wrong. But the Greeks, who invented iambic pentameter, used it as a dance beat. Later writers no longer used it as something one could literally shimmy to, but it was still a way to organize the rhythmic noise and swing of speech. An *iamb* contains one unaccented (or unstressed) syllable and one accented (stressed) syllable, in that order. It borrows from the natural swing of our heartbeats to go *ker-THUMP, ker-THUMP.* Five of these ker-thumping units in a row make a line of iambic *penta*meter.

Dance or rock music needs a good, regular thumping of drums (or drum machine) and bass to get our feet tapping and bodies dancing, but things can get awfully monotonous if that's all there is to the sound. Poetry works the same way. With its ten syllables and five ker-thumps, a line like "he WENT to TOWN toDAY to BUY a CAR" is perfect iambic pentameter. It's just as regular as a metronome. But it isn't poetry. "In SOOTH/ I KNOW/ not WHY/ I AM/ so SAD" is poetry (*The Merchant of Venice,* Act 1, Scene 1). Writers like Shakespeare change the iambic pentameter pattern of their blank verse all the time to keep things sounding interesting. The melody of vowels and other sound effects makes the lines even more musical and varied. As it reaches the audience's ears, this mix of basic, patterned beat and sound variations carries powerful messages of meaning and emotion. The beating, regular rhythms of blank verse also help actors remember their lines.

Why did Shakespeare use this form? Blank verse dominated through a combination of novelty, tradition, and ease. The Greeks and Romans passed on a tradition of combining poetry and drama. English playwrights experimented with this tradition by using all sorts of verse and prose for their plays. By the 1590s, blank verse had caught on with some of the best new writers in London. In the hands of writers like the popular Christopher Marlowe and the up-and-coming Will Shakespeare, it was more than just the latest craze in on-stage sound.

Blank verse also fit well with the English language itself. Compared to languages like French and Italian, English is hard to rhyme. It's also heavily accentual—another way of saying that English really bumps and thumps.

The words and sounds coming from the stage were new and thrilling to Shakespeare's audience. England was falling in love with its own language. English speakers were still making up grammar, spelling, and pronunciation as they went along—giving the language more of a "hands-on" feel than it has today. The grammar books and dictionaries that finally fixed the "rules" of English did not appear until after Shakespeare's death. The language grew and grew, soaking up words from other languages, combining and making new words. Politically, the country also grew in power and pride.

Shakespeare's language reflects this sense of freedom, experimentation, and power. When he put his words in the beat of blank verse and the mouths of London's best actors, it must have sounded a little like the birth of rock and roll—mixing old styles and new sounds to make a new, triumphant swagger.

Publishing Shakespeare

Books of Shakespeare's plays come in all shapes and sizes. They range from slim paperbacks like this one to heavy, muscle-building anthologies of his collected works. Libraries devote shelves of space to works by and about "the Bard." Despite all that paper and ink, no printed text of a Shakespeare play can claim to be an exact, word-by-word copy of what Shakespeare wrote.

Today, most writers work on computers and can save their work electronically. Students everywhere know the horror of losing the only copy of something they've written and make sure they always have a backup version! In Shakespeare's time, a playwright delivered a handwritten copy of his work to the acting company that asked him to write a play. This may have been his only copy—which was now the property of the company, not the writer. In general, plays were viewed as mere "entertainments"—not literary art. They were written quickly and were often disposed of when the acting companies had no more use for them.

The draft Shakespeare delivered was a work in progress. He and the company probably added, deleted, and changed some material—stage directions, entrances and exits, even lines and character names—during rehearsals. Companies may have had a clean copy written out by a scribe (a professional hand-writer) or by the writer himself. Most likely they kept this house copy for future performances. No copies of Shakespeare's plays in his own handwriting have survived.

Acting companies might perform a hit play for years before it was printed, usually in small books called *quartos*. However, the first published versions of Shakespeare's plays vary considerably. Some of these texts are thought to be of an inferior, incomplete quality. Because of this, scholars have speculated that they are not based on authoritative, written copies, but were re-created from actors' memories or from the shorthand notes of a scribe working for a publisher.

Shakespearean scholars often call these apparently faulty versions of his plays "bad quartos." Why might such texts have appeared? Scholars have guessed that they are "pirated versions." They believe that acting companies tried to keep their plays out of print to prevent rival troupes from stealing popular material. However, booksellers sometimes printed unauthorized versions of Shakespeare's plays that were used by competing companies. The pirated versions may have been done with help from actors who had played minor roles in the play, memorized it, and then sold their unreliable, memorized versions. (In recent years, this theory has been challenged by some scholars who argue that the "bad" quartos may be based on Shakespeare's own first drafts or that they reliably reflect early performance texts of the plays.)

"Good" quartos were printed with the permission of the company that owned the play and were based on written copies. However, even these authorized versions were far from perfect. The printers had to work either by deciphering the playwright's handwriting or by using a flawed version printed earlier. They also had to memorize lines as they manually set type on the press. And they decided how a line should be punctuated and spelled—not always with foolproof judgment!

The first full collection of Shakespeare's plays came out in 1623, seven years after his death. Called the "First Folio," this collection included 36 plays compiled by John Heminge and Henry Condell, actor-friends of Shakespeare from The King's Men troupe.

To develop the First Folio texts, Heminge, Condell, and their co-editors probably worked with a mix of handwritten and both good and bad printed versions of their friend's plays. Their 1623 version had many errors, and though later editions of that text corrected some mistakes, they also added new ones. The First Folio also contained no indications of where acts and scenes began and ended. The scene and act divisions that appear standard in most modern editions of Shakespeare actually rely on the shrewd guesses of generations of editors and researchers.

Most modern editors of Shakespeare depend on a combination of trustworthy early publications to come up with the most accurate text possible. They often use the versions in the First Folio, its later editions, and other "good," authorized publications of single plays. In some cases, they also consult "bad" versions or rely on pure guesswork to decide the most likely reading of some words or lines. Because of such uncertainties, modern editions of Shakespeare often vary, depending on editors' research and choices. This version of William Shakespeare's *Macbeth* is taken from the Folio Edition of 1623.

Macbeth

Introduction to the Play

Suppose you were asked to write a story or play about evil. Would you fill your work with terrifying and unusual sights and sounds—blood-curdling screams, gruesome acts, fearsome ghosts? Or would you show a seemingly peaceful, sunny neighborhood somewhere, where evil hides behind common choices and surfaces?

At first glance, *Macbeth* seems to have everything in common with the first option and nothing with the second. Shakespeare's play features witches' sabbaths, bloody violence, and a ghost. Dominated by dark and gloomy settings, it describes a natural world where predators and chaos reign, while innocence and order shrink in fear. Everything about this world seems extraordinary—and in the worst way.

The main figure in this world is Macbeth, a usurping king from Scottish history. At first glance, he too is no ordinary figure. Macbeth is a prominent member of what seems like a rather exotic society: a warrior culture of the distant past. Shakespeare surrounds him with chilling forces—from the witches' prophecies to his ruthless wife. And yet Macbeth is not *simply* a monster. He is not just the oversized villain of a swift, bloody tale. Macbeth's struggles to overcome his feelings of temptation, despair, and guilt are portrayed just as vividly as his evil acts, and this makes him a very human villain.

Watching and hearing the torments of Macbeth and his wife, Shakespeare's audiences remember their own struggles with weakness and temptation. We recall how our own choices may have trapped us in destructive paths. In this way, Macbeth is *almost* like someone we might know. He is *almost* sympathetic, *almost* just like us. Terrifyingly, he is also almost what we might become—especially if we lived in the strange, dramatic world of the stage.

This combination of the recognizable and the unfamiliar makes *Macbeth* one of Shakespeare's greatest works of tragic art. If audiences did not see some of their everyday selves in Macbeth and Lady Macbeth, the play would not be nearly so moving—or so frightening. Shakespeare shows us some horrible results of what we know to be very common evils: basic emotions like ambition, envy, anger, greed, and fear.

Although Macbeth is in some ways a universal character, most scholars believe that Shakespeare wrote the play in part to please just one person. This was James I, England's monarch from 1603 to 1625. In Shakespeare's play, the defeat of Macbeth's evil rule is linked to the rise of James's family line. The witches' prominence in the play seems to reflect and flatter James's own interest in witchcraft and the supernatural. References to a form of deceptive speech called *equivocation* probably allude to the Gunpowder Plot, an attempt to assassinate James and members of his government that occurred in 1605. Because of these apparent links to James and his reign, scholars usually date *Macbeth*'s first performance at The Globe around 1606–1607. (Look for more on the play's links to James in the introductory material before each act.)

Macbeth is sometimes called the last of Shakespeare's "four great tragedies"—*Hamlet* (c. 1599–1601), *Othello* (c. 1603–1604), *King Lear* (c. 1605–1606), and *Macbeth*. The four plays are grouped together partly because they all take a dark look at human nature. All four focus on the causes and effects of evil. However, they also differ in important ways. For example, *Macbeth* is much shorter than *Hamlet,* and it also features far less prose. Almost all of *Macbeth* is written in poetry, and it is often considered one of the greatest examples of Shakespeare's powers as a poet. Much of the play's urgent quality comes from its *sound. Macbeth* repeatedly grabs its audience's attention through their *ears,* with lines that range from dense blank verse to the witches' singsong chants—which sound almost like sinister nursery rhymes.

Macbeth's wonderful poetry is also filled with striking images. It is deeply affecting (and frightening) because of its close relationship to a primitive natural world. As you read *Macbeth,* notice how frequently Shakespeare mentions the animal world or uses images of time and of colors (such as white, green, and especially red) to tell us something about the state of Macbeth's mind or his society.

Macbeth is a sophisticated play, full of complexity and depth. Many readers have found life lessons in the play regarding complicated matters, such as the meaning of free will. But *Macbeth* gains much of its power by drawing images from a raw natural world and from ancient childhood emotions—such as fear of the dark. Like the witches' brew, Shakespeare's images combine raw ingredients to create powerful, profound, and terrifying effects.

Macbeth's Sources

Fact or fiction? *Macbeth* deals with some real-life figures from Scottish history, including Shakespeare's title character. There really was a King Macbeth, who ruled Scotland from 1040 to 1057. Nevertheless, it's best to think twice before citing Shakespeare as an expert in your history exam.

While writing *Macbeth*, Shakespeare apparently turned to the 1587 edition of *Chronicles of England, Scotlande, and Irelande*, a popular work by the English historian Raphael Holinshed. Several key episodes in *Macbeth* are based on Holinshed's account, including Macbeth's encounters with witches and witchcraft. However, Holinshed's story of Macbeth's rule also differs from Shakespeare's play in important ways. According to Holinshed, Macbeth gained the throne after defeating his cousin Duncan in battle, and he was supported by Banquo in doing so. When Shakespeare wrote the section relating how Macbeth obtained the throne, he incorporated details from an entirely different story in the *Chronicles*. This story tells of how Scotland's King Duff was murdered by one Donwald and his wife.

The historical accuracy of the play is questionable for another reason. Scholars today don't think of Holinshed as a particularly solid recorder of history. They point out that not all of Holinshed's own sources were particularly trustworthy. This isn't just because Holinshed's tale of Macbeth features witches! It also promoted such false notions as the idea that England's James I was descended from Banquo through Banquo's son, Fleance. In *Macbeth*, Shakespeare alludes to this genealogy, which is now known to be fictitious.

Although Shakespeare frequently "borrowed" heavily from other sources to create his plots, it can sometimes be very interesting to see what he left out. Contrary to Holinshed's version, Shakespeare has made Banquo guiltless in Duncan's death. He greatly enlarges Lady Macbeth's role, compresses the time of Macbeth's reign, and adds such new features as Banquo's ghost. In watching how Shakespeare changes, adds, and omits material in his source stories, we see a great dramatic mind at work, shaping his plays' unforgettable conflicts and characters.

Although Holinshed's *Chronicles* gave Shakespeare most of his background for *Macbeth*, critics have also detected the influences of other possible sources. These include George Buchanan's history book *Rerum Scotarium Historia* (1582, written in Latin); the memoirs of the Renaissance scholar Erasmus; and works by the Roman playwright Seneca (4 B.C. (?)–A.D. 65)—especially an early seventeenth-century

English version of Seneca's play *Medea.* Sources on witchcraft may have included reports of Scottish witch trials published around 1590, as well as King James's own book on witchcraft, titled *Daemonology* (1597).

The Text of *Macbeth*

Macbeth was first published in the First Folio (see "Publishing Shakespeare") in 1623. It appears to have been taken from a text used by Shakespeare's company, The King's Men.

   Macbeth is the shortest of all Shakespeare's tragedies. Because of this, some scholars believe that the First Folio version reflects cuts made by Shakespeare's company to a longer original. While it appears that companies often made alterations to plays to shorten or enhance the action on stage, some Shakespeare experts have suggested that the First Folio *Macbeth* was cut to fit the demands of one particular, special performance or because of censorship. This cannot be definitively proved, however.

   Another oddity of *Macbeth*'s text can be found in the scenes that feature Hecate, the witch goddess. Most scholars assume that all of Act 3, Scene 5 and parts of Act 4, Scene 1 were not written by Shakespeare. These sections include songs from *The Witch,* a play by Thomas Middleton written sometime between 1609 and 1620. Middleton or another writer may also have written the dialogue passages that do not seem to be Shakespeare's. Most scholars assume that these alterations and additions were made to *Macbeth* by The King's Men after Shakespeare retired from active involvement with the company.

Macbeth

Original text and modern version

Characters

Duncan King of Scotland

Malcolm
Donalbain } his sons

Macbeth Thane of Glamis and a general in Duncan's army, later king

Banquo a general in Duncan's army, Macbeth's friend

Macduff a Scots nobleman, loyal to Scotland

Lennox
Ross
Mentieth } Scots noblemen
Angus
Caithness

Fleance Banquo's son

Siward Earl of Northumberland

Young Siward Siward's son

Seton Macbeth's personal officer

Macduff's son

An English doctor

A Scottish doctor

A sergeant

A porter

An old man

Three Murderers

Lady Macbeth

Lady Macduff

A lady-in-waiting

Three Witches

Hecate

Apparitions

Lords, Gentlemen, Officers, Soldiers, Attendants, and Messengers

All the World's a Stage Introduction

Get ready for shrieks and spells—but don't mistake this world of witches and apparitions for Halloween! *Macbeth* is a very dark play. The action deals with witchcraft and murder. Key events occur at night, often in dark and gloomy places. The very first scene takes place on a storm-swept waste, just before a battle. The forces of Duncan, the King of Scotland, are fighting rebels led by a chieftain named Macdonwald and an invading army headed by the King of Norway. A traitor also exists within his own ranks—the Thane of Cawdor. Two thanes support King Duncan, Macbeth, and Banquo. Both are also generals in Duncan's army.

Macbeth is set in medieval Scotland. Macbeth, Banquo, Duncan, and Malcolm are historical figures, but for the sake of the play, Shakespeare did not stick to the facts. Instead, Duncan is an elderly king beloved by his people. Also, the Lady Macbeth of history was much less important to the events that unfolded than the Lady Macbeth of the play.

What's in a Name? Characters

Macbeth dominates the action and delivers a third of the play's lines. In this warrior society, he is a ferocious fighter. But you may also notice that Macbeth's personality definitely has a downside—his ambition. Macbeth makes speeches and remarks to himself that share his private emotions and visions with the audience. The longer speeches are *soliloquies,* while shorter comments are *asides.* Through them you learn how Macbeth feels about the events going on around him.

Macbeth also shares his feelings with his wife, Lady Macbeth. We'll also observe Macbeth's co-commander, Banquo. His watchfulness keeps us alert, too. He, too, is strong and brave, but he differs from Macbeth in important ways.

Three characters are just as odd as they are important—the Three Witches. They are the first people we see, calling to each other through a thunderstorm and preparing to meet Macbeth. Helped by their "familiars"—evil spirits that take the form of animals such as cats, toads, or bats—the Witches are not to be taken lightly. They have the gift of prophecy, and when they tell Macbeth that he will be king, Macbeth must take them seriously.

COME WHAT MAY Things to Watch For

It's no accident that *Macbeth's* first scene takes place in a thunderstorm. Throughout the play, nature is behaving in frightening and strange ways. And by *nature* Shakespeare doesn't just mean the weather.

For example, do the female characters fit stereotypical feminine qualities that are sometimes called "natural"—traits like weakness and nurturing instincts?

An important image in *Macbeth* is chanted by the Witches: "Fair is foul, and foul is fair" (1, 1, 12). Again and again, what *seems* to be a good thing—Duncan's reward to Macbeth for defeating the Thane of Cawdor—is actually a terrible thing. It convinces Macbeth that the Witches spoke truly—he will be king. His ambition is encouraged, and any sense of order in the kingdom is destroyed.

All Our Yesterdays Historical and Social Context

Witchcraft wasn't just Halloween fun or Hollywood shivers for Elizabethans. People lived in daily fear of dark forces. They believed that witches could make humans and animals ill or even die and control the weather. Those accused of witchcraft faced terrible punishments.

The Play's the Thing Staging

Watch out! Shakespeare's company certainly knew how to start things with a bang. To make the sound of thunder in *Macbeth*'s first scene, they rolled cannon balls behind and above the stage. They may have used fireworks to create the effect of lightning. Using a balcony entrance above the stage and a trapdoor in the center may have helped the Witches appear and disappear.

Trapdoors and balconies weren't the only tricky exits and entrances. Shakespeare often timed entrances to make a point. Throughout *Macbeth*, watch for what people are saying just before a character appears. For example, Duncan talks about another character's disloyalty just before Macbeth enters. Is this timing a bad sign for the Scottish king?

My Words Fly Up Language

The Three Witches are also known as the "Weird Sisters." *Weird* comes from an Old English word meaning "fate," so the Witches' name connects them with the idea of destiny.

The Witches also talk in a strange manner. Often, they seem to say things that seem unclear or paradoxical. *Paradoxes* are statements that seem contradictory but that contain a truth. The Witches like to talk in this tricky way.

Occasionally, Shakespeare refers to proverbial sayings that are lost to modern-day audiences. In Scene 7, Lady Macbeth insults her husband by referring to an old proverb, or "adage," about a cat. The full saying goes, "The cat would eat fish, but would not wet her feet." In other words, the cat didn't want to do the dirty work of catching her meal!

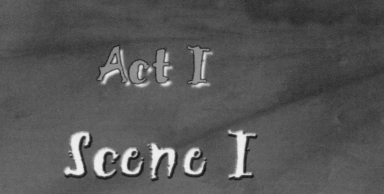

Act I

Scene I

*A desert place. Thunder and lightning. Enter three **Witches**.*

1st Witch   When shall we three meet again
  In thunder, lightning, or in rain?

2nd Witch   When the hurlyburly's done,
  When the battle's lost and won.

5 **3rd Witch**   That will be ere the set of sun.

1st Witch   Where the place?

2nd Witch   Upon the heath.

3rd Witch   There to meet with Macbeth.

1st Witch   I come, Graymalkin!

10 **2nd Witch**   Paddock calls.

3rd Witch   Anon!

All   Fair is foul, and foul is fair:
  Hover through the fog and filthy air.

[*They vanish*]

An empty field during a storm. Thunder and lightning. Three **Witches** *enter.*

1st Witch   When shall the three of us meet again? In thunder, lightning, and rain?

2nd Witch   When the trouble is all done; when the battle's lost and won.

3rd Witch   Before the setting of the sun.

1st Witch   Where is the place?

2nd Witch   In the fields.

3rd Witch   There we will meet Macbeth.

1st Witch   I'm coming, my Gray Cat!

2nd Witch   My Toad calls me.

3rd Witch   I'm coming!

All   Fair is foul and foul is fair. Hover through the fog and filthy air.

[They disappear]

Act I

Scene II

A camp near Forres. Alarum. Enter **King Duncan, Malcolm, Donalbain, Lennox,** *with attendants, meeting a bleeding* **Sergeant.**

Duncan   What bloody man is that? He can report,
As seemeth by his plight, of the revolt
The newest state.

Malcolm   This is the sergeant,
5   Who like a good and hardy soldier fought
'Gainst my captivity . . . Hail, brave friend!
Say to the king the knowledge of the broil
As thou didst leave it.

Sergeant   Doubtful it stood;
10   As two spent swimmers that do cling together
And choke their art . . . The merciless Macdonwald –
Worthy to be a rebel, for to that
The multiplying villainies of nature
Do swarm upon him – from the Western Isles
15   Of kerns and gallowglasses is supplied;
And Fortune, on his damned quarrel smiling,
Showed like a rebel's whore: but all's too weak:
For brave Macbeth – well he deserves that name –
Disdaining fortune, with his brandished steel,
20   Which smoked with bloody execution,
Like Valour's minion carved out his passage

An army camp near Forres, a town in Scotland. A trumpet blows.
King Duncan; *his sons* **Malcolm** *and* **Donalbain;** *and* **Lennox**
enter with their servants. They meet a wounded **Sergeant.**

Duncan Who is that wounded man? Since his wounds seem
fresh, he should be able to give us the latest news of the
battle.

Malcolm This is the sergeant who fought so hard and well to
keep me from being captured. Greetings, my brave friend!
Tell the king how the battle was going when you left it.

Sergeant The outcome was doubtful. The armies were like two
swimmers who are so tired they hang onto one another until
they sink. The cruel rebel leader, Macdonwald—who brings
more and more evil swarming around him—has hired
foot soldiers and horsemen from the Western Isles as
reinforcements. Fickle luck seemed to be on his side at first,
but not for long. For Macbeth—who deserves to be called
brave—cared nothing for luck. Waving his blood-stained
sword, he cut his way through the rebels until he reached

Till he faced the slave;
Which ne'er shook hands, nor bade farewell to him,
Till he unseamed him from the nave to the chops,
25   And fixed his head upon our battlements.

Duncan O, valiant cousin! worthy gentleman!

Sergeant As whence the sun 'gins his reflection
Shipwracking storms and direful thunders break;
So from that spring whence comfort seemed to come
30   Discomfort swells. Mark, king of Scotland, mark!
No sooner justice had, with valour armed,
Compelled these skipping kerns to trust their heels,
But the Norweyan lord, surveying vantage,
With furbished arms and new supplies of men,
35   Began a fresh assault.

Duncan   Dismayed not this
Our captains, Macbeth and Banquo?

Sergeant   Yes;
As sparrows, eagles; or the hare, the lion:
40   If I say sooth, I must report they were
As cannons overcharged with double cracks,
So they doubly redoubled strokes upon the foe:
Except they meant to bathe in reeking wounds,
Or memorize another Golgotha,
45   I cannot tell:
But I am faint, my gashes cry for help.

Duncan So well thy words become thee, as thy wounds;
They smack of honour both. Go get him surgeons.

[*Exit* **Sergeant,** *attended*]

Who comes here?

[*Enter* **Ross** *and* **Angus**]

Macdonwald. Macbeth didn't stop to greet him. He carved the rebel leader open from his middle to his jaws, chopped off his head, and stuck it on our walls.

Duncan   Oh brave cousin! Worthy gentleman!

Sergeant   But just as a spring day can bring storms, trouble followed. Listen carefully, King of Scotland! No sooner had our good, brave men forced the rebels to take to their heels in retreat, than the King of Norway saw his opportunity. He began a new attack with fresh, well-armed soldiers.

Duncan   Weren't our commanders, Macbeth and Banquo, frightened by this?

Sergeant   They were as frightened as eagles are of sparrows or as lions are of rabbits. They were like cannons firing double loads of gunpowder. They fought doubly hard against these new enemies. I can't tell whether they wanted to swim in blood or make this battlefield as famous as Golgotha. But now I'm feeling weak. My wounds need to be treated.

Duncan   Both your report and your wounds do you credit. Get him a doctor.

[*The* **Sergeant** *is helped off*]

Who is this coming?

[**Ross** *and* **Angus** *enter*]

50 **Malcolm**   The worthy thane of Ross.

Lennox   What a haste looks through his eyes! So should he
        look
     That seems to speak things strange.

Ross   God save the king!

55 **Duncan**   Whence cam'st thou, worthy thane?

Ross   From Fife, great king,
     Where the Norweyan banners flout the sky,
     And fan our people cold.
     Norway himself, with terrible numbers,
60   Assisted by the most disloyal traitor
     The thane of Cawdor, began a dismal conflict,
     Till that Bellona's bridegroom, lapped in proof,
     Confronted him with self-comparisons,
     Point against point, rebellious arm 'gainst arm,
65   Curbing his lavish spirit: and, to conclude,
     The victory fell on us.

Duncan   Great happiness!

Ross   That now
     Sweno, the Norways' king, craves composition;
70   Nor would we deign him burial of his men
     Till he disbursed, at Saint Colme's Inch,
     Ten thousand dollars to our general use.

Duncan   No more that thane of Cawdor shall deceive
     Our bosom interest: go pronounce his present death,
75   And with his former title greet Macbeth.

Ross   I'll see it done.

Duncan   What he hath lost, noble Macbeth hath won.

                              [*Exeunt*]

Malcolm The good thane of Ross.

Lennox From the look in his eyes, he seems to be in a great hurry, as if he had something important to tell us.

Ross God save the King!

Duncan Where are you coming from, good thane?

Ross From Fife, great King, where the Norwegians struck icy terror in our troops. The King of Norway himself, aided by that traitor the thane of Cawdor, led a great army against us in a fearful attack. But Macbeth was a match for the Norwegian king! Armored like the bridegroom of the war goddess herself, Macbeth fought the King hand to hand, until he forced him to yield. So in the end, we were victorious!

Duncan Wonderful!

Ross And now the Norwegian king, Sweno, is asking for a peace treaty. We refused to let him bury his dead until he had paid us a huge sum of money at Inchcolme.

Duncan The thane of Cawdor shall not betray us again. Go and see to it that he is put to death at once. Give his title to Macbeth when you find him.

Ross It will be done.

Duncan What Cawdor has lost, noble Macbeth has won.

[*They exit*]

Act I

Scene III

A heath. Thunder. Enter the three **Witches.**

1st Witch   Where hast thou been, sister?

2nd Witch   Killing swine.

3rd Witch   Sister, where thou?

1st Witch   A sailor's wife had chestnuts in her lap,
5   And munched, and munched, and munched: 'Give me',
         quoth I.
     'Aroint thee, witch!' the rump-fed ronyon cries.
     Her husband's to Aleppo gone, master o'th' Tiger:
     But in a sieve I'll thither sail,
10   And, like a rat without a tail,
     I'll do, I'll do, and I'll do.

2nd Witch   I'll give thee a wind.

1st Witch   Th'art kind.

3rd Witch   And I another.

15   **1st Witch**   I myself have all the other,
     And the very ports they blow,
     All the quarters that they know
     I'th' shipman's card.
     I will drain him dry as hay:
20   Sleep shall neither night nor day
     Hang upon his pent-house lid;
     He shall live a man forbid:

An empty field. Thunder. The three **Witches** *enter.*

1st Witch Where have you been, sister?

2nd Witch Killing pigs.

3rd Witch Sister, where have you been?

1st Witch A sailor's wife had some chestnuts in her lap. She munched and munched and munched. "Give me some," I said. "Get out of here, witch!" the fat, ugly thing cried. Her husband is captain of the *Tiger,* sailing to the East. I'll sail after him in a sieve, and like a rat without a tail I'll make trouble, trouble, trouble.

2nd Witch I'll give you a wind to help blow you there.

1st Witch Thank you.

3rd Witch And I'll give you another wind.

1st Witch I myself control all the other winds that blow from every port and direction of the compass. I'll drain him dry as hay, making him suffer from thirst. Day or night, he won't close his eyes to sleep. He'll live under my curse.

Weary se'nights nine times nine
Shall he dwindle, peak, and pine:
25 Though his bark cannot be lost,
Yet it shall be tempest-tost.
Look what I have.

2nd Witch Show me, show me.

1st Witch Here I have a pilot's thumb,
30 Wrecked as homeward he did come.

[*Drum within*]

3rd Witch A drum, a drum!
Macbeth doth come.

All The Weird Sisters, hand in hand,
Posters of the sea and land,
35 Thus do go, about, about,
Thrice to thine, and thrice to mine,
And thrice again, to make up nine.
Peace! the charm's wound up.

[*Enter* **Macbeth** *and* **Banquo**]

Macbeth So foul and fair a day I have not seen.

40 **Banquo** How far is't called to Forres? What are these,
So withered, and so wild in their attire,
That look not like th'inhabitants o'th'earth,
And yet are on't? Live you? or are you aught
That man may question? You seem to understand me,
45 By each at once her choppy finger laying
Upon her skinny lips: you should be women,
And yet your beards forbid me to interpret
That you are so.

Macbeth Speak, if you can: what are you?

For nine-times-nine weary weeks, he'll shrink and suffer.
Though I may not sink his ship, I will batter it with storms.
Look what I have.

2nd Witch Show me, show me.

1st Witch This is the thumb of a ship's pilot who was drowned sailing home.

[*A drum beats*]

3rd Witch I hear a drumming. Macbeth is coming.

All [*chanting*] The Weird Sisters, hand in hand, swift travelers of the sea and land, go round and round this way. Three times toward yours, and three times toward mine, and three more times to make up nine. Enough! The charm is done.

[**Macbeth** *and* **Banquo** *enter*]

Macbeth I have never seen a day that was so foul and so fair.

Banquo How far is it to Forres? What are these creatures that are so wrinkled and so strangely dressed? That don't look like anything that would live on earth, but there they are. [*To the* **Witches**] Are you alive? Are you anything that a man can speak to? You seem to understand me, because each of you is placing a scaly finger on her skinny lips. You seem to be women, but you have beards.

Macbeth Speak, if you can. What are you?

1st Witch All hail, Macbeth! hail to thee, thane of Glamis!   50

2nd Witch All hail, Macbeth! hail to thee, thane of Cawdor!

3rd Witch All hail, Macbeth! that shalt be king hereafter.

Banquo Good sir, why do you start, and seem to fear
    Things that do sound so fair? I'th' name of truth,
    Are ye fantastical, or that indeed   55
    Which outwardly ye show? My noble partner
    You greet with present grace and great prediction
    Of noble having and of royal hope,
    That he seems rapt withall: to me you speak not.
    If you can look into the seeds of time,   60
    And say which grain will grow and which will not,
    Speak then to me, who neither beg nor fear
    Your favours nor your hate.

1st Witch Hail!

2nd Witch Hail!   65

3rd Witch Hail!

1st Witch Lesser than Macbeth, and greater.

2nd Witch Not so happy, yet much happier.

3rd Witch Thou shalt get kings, though thou be none:
    So all hail, Macbeth and Banquo!   70

1st Witch Banquo and Macbeth, all hail!

Macbeth Stay, you imperfect speakers, tell me more:
    By Sinel's death I know I am thane of Glamis;
    But how of Cawdor? the thane of Cawdor lives
    A prosperous gentleman; and to be king   75
    Stands not within the prospect of belief,
    No more than to be Cawdor. Say from whence
    You owe this strange intelligence, or why
    Upon this blasted heath you stop our way
    With such prophetic greeting? Speak, I charge you.   80

1st Witch All hail, Macbeth! Hail to you, thane of Glamis!

2nd Witch All hail, Macbeth! Hail to you, thane of Cawdor!

3rd Witch All hail, Macbeth! In the future, you shall be king!

Banquo [*to* **Macbeth**] Good sir, why are you so startled? Why does what sounds so good seem to frighten you? [*To the* **Witches**] Tell me the truth. Am I dreaming or are you as human as you appear? You greet my noble friend with both his present title and a new honor and predict he will be king. Now he's absorbed in thoughts about this. You say nothing to me. If you can see the future—what will come to be and what will not—speak to me, then. I don't beg for your good will or fear your hatred.

1st Witch Hail!

2nd Witch Hail!

3rd Witch Hail!

1st Witch Both lesser than Macbeth and greater.

2nd Witch Not so happy, yet much happier.

3rd Witch You will not be a king, but your children will be kings.

1st Witch Banquo and Macbeth, all hail!

Macbeth Wait, you vague speakers. Tell me more. I know that my father Sinel's death made me thane of Glamis. But how can I be thane of Cawdor? The thane of Cawdor is still alive. He is a prosperous gentleman. It is simply unbelievable that I could become king—as unbelievable as that I could become thane of Cawdor. Tell us where you got this strange news. Tell us why you stop and greet us on this wasteland with these predictions. Speak, I order you!

[They vanish]

Banquo The earth hath bubbles, as the water has,
And these are of them: whither are they vanished?

Macbeth Into the air; and what seemed corporal, melted,
As breath into the wind. Would they had stayed!

85 **Banquo** Were such things here as we do speak about?
Or have we eaten on the insane root
That takes the reason prisoner?

Macbeth Your children shall be kings.

Banquo   You shall be king.

90 **Macbeth** 'And thane of Cawdor too: went it not so?

Banquo To th'selfsame tune and words. Who's here?

*[Enter **Ross** and **Angus**]*

Ross The king hath happily received, Macbeth,
The news of thy success: and when he reads
Thy personal venture in the rebels' fight,
95 His wonders and his praises do contend
Which should be thine or his: silenced with that,
In viewing o'er the rest o'th' self-same day,
He finds thee in the stout Norweyan ranks,
Nothing afeard of what thyself didst make
100 Strange images of death. As thick as hail
Came post with post, and every one did bear
Thy praises in his kingdom's great defence,
And poured them down before him.

Angus   We are sent
105 To give thee from our royal master thanks,
Only to herald thee into his sight,
Not pay thee.

[*The* **Witches** *disappear*]

Banquo The earth must produce bubbles, just like water does. These creatures must have been such bubbles. Where did they go?

Macbeth Into the air. They seemed like something you could touch, but they disappeared, melted, just like breath disappears in the wind. I wish they had stayed!

Banquo Were these creatures we are speaking of really here? Or have we gone mad and hallucinated them?

Macbeth Your children shall be kings.

Banquo You shall be king.

Macbeth And thane of Cawdor too. Isn't that what they said?

Banquo That's just what they said. Who's here?

[**Ross** *and* **Angus** *enter*]

Ross Macbeth, the news of your success made the King very happy. When he read of your personal bravery in fighting the rebels, his admiration overcame his desire to praise you. He was speechless. Later the same day, he learned how you charged in among the tough Norwegian soldiers. You killed others, but death did not frighten you at all. Thick as a hailstorm, messenger after messenger came to the King. They poured in with reports, all praising of your actions to defend his kingdom.

Angus The King has sent us to give you his thanks. But our role is only to bring you to him, not to reward you.

Ross   And for an earnest of a greater honour,
He bade me, from him, call thee thane of Cawdor:
110   In which addition, hail, most worthy thane,
For it is thine.

Banquo   [*Aside*]   What, can the devil speak true?

Macbeth   The thane of Cawdor lives: why do you dress me
In borrowed robes?

115 **Angus**   Who was the thane lives yet,
But under heavy judgement bears that life
Which he deserves to lose. Whether he was combined
With those of Norway, or did line the rebel
With hidden help and vantage, or that with both
120   He laboured in his country's wreck, I know not;
But treasons capital, confessed, and proved,
Have overthrown him.

Macbeth   [*Aside*]   Glamis, and thane of Cawdor:
The greatest is behind. Thanks for your pains –
125   [*To* **Banquo**]   Do you not hope your children shall be kings,
When those that gave the thane of Cawdor to me
Promised no less to them?

Banquo   [*To* **Macbeth**]   That, trusted home,
Might yet enkindle you unto the crown,
130   Besides the thane of Cawdor. But 'tis strange:
And oftentimes, to win us to our harm,
The instruments of darkness tell us truths,
Win us with honest trifles, to betray's
In deepest consequence.
135   Cousins, a word, I pray you.

Macbeth   [*Aside*]   Two truths are told,
As happy prologues to the swelling act
Of the imperial theme. I thank you, gentlemen.
This supernatural soliciting
140   Cannot be ill; cannot be good. If ill,

Ross As a pledge of future honors, the King ordered me to call you thane of Cawdor. Hail, most worthy thane, this title is now yours.

Banquo [*to himself*] What, can the devil speak the truth?

Macbeth The thane of Cawdor is still alive. Why do you dress me in borrowed robes?

Angus The man who was formerly the thane of Cawdor is still alive, but he is under a sentence of death, which he fully deserves. I don't know whether he was helping the forces of the King of Norway or secretly assisting the rebels. Perhaps he was working with both to destroy his country. But he has confessed his treason, it has been proved, and he deserves death. He is finished.

Macbeth [*to himself*] I'm thane of Glamis and now will be thane of Cawdor. And the greatest prediction is still to come. [*To* **Ross** *and* **Angus**] Thank you for taking this trouble. [*To* **Banquo**] Don't you hope now that your children will be kings, since that was the prediction of those creatures that promised I would be thane of Cawdor?

Banquo [*to* **Macbeth**] If we trust their predictions all the way, it might in the future arouse your desire to be king. What has happened is strange, but the forces of evil often tell us truths in order to tempt us. They win our confidence in small matters in order to betray us in the most serious ones.
[*To* **Ross** *and* **Angus**] My lords, please let me speak with you.

Macbeth [*to himself*] Two of the things I was told have come true, like the pleasant opening of a drama in which I become king. [*To* **Ross** *and* **Angus**] Thank you, gentlemen. [*To himself*] This supernatural temptation cannot be evil and cannot be good. If it is evil, why has it given me a pledge

Why hath it given me earnest of success,
Commencing in a truth? I am Thane of Cawdor.
If good, why do I yield to that suggestion
Whose horrid image doth unfix my hair,
145 And make my seated heart knock at my ribs,
Against the use of nature? Present fears
Are less than horrible imaginings:
My thought, whose murder yet is but fantastical,
Shakes so my single state of man that function
150 Is smothered in surmise, and nothing is
But what is not.

Banquo   Look how our partner's rapt.

Macbeth [*Aside*] If chance will have me king, why,
        chance may crown me,
155 Without my stir.

Banquo   New honours come upon him,
    Like our strange garments, cleave not to their mould
    But with the aid of use.

Macbeth   Come what come may,
160 Time and the hour runs through the roughest day.

Banquo Worthy Macbeth, we stay upon your leisure.

Macbeth Give me your favour: my dull brain was wrought
    With things forgotten. Kind gentlemen, your pains
    Are registered where every day I turn
165 The leaf to read them . . . Let us toward the king.
    Think upon what hath chanced: and at more time,
    The interim having weighed it, let us speak
    Our free hearts each to other.

Banquo   Very gladly.

170 **Macbeth** Till then, enough. Come, friends.

[*Exeunt*]

of future success by telling me the truth at the outset? I am thane of Cawdor. If it is good, why am I thinking thoughts so horrible that they make my hair stand on end and my heart beat so hard it knocks against my ribs? Horrors in the imagination are worse than fears of real things. Just the thought of committing murder so defeats my weak nature that all action is overcome by imagination. Only the things I'm imagining seem real.

Banquo [*to* **Ross** *and* **Angus**] Look how carried away our friend is.

Macbeth [*to himself*] If fate means me to be king, then fate may crown me without any act on my part.

Banquo [*to* **Ross** *and* **Angus**] Macbeth's new honors are like new clothes, which don't fit properly until they've been worn a bit.

Macbeth [*to himself*] Whatever may come, the roughest day finally passes.

Banquo Worthy Macbeth, we're ready when you are.

Macbeth Please excuse me. My dull brain was preoccupied with some matters I had forgotten. Kind gentlemen, what you have done for me is recorded in my memory. Let us go to meet the King. [*To* **Banquo**] Think about what has happened. And when we have had some time to consider these events, let's share our feelings.

Banquo Very gladly.

Macbeth Until then, enough. Come friends.

[*They exit*]

Act I

Scene IV

Forres. The Palace. Flourish. Enter **King Duncan, Malcolm, Donalbain, Lennox,** *and* **Attendants.**

Duncan   Is execution done on Cawdor? Are not
Those in commission yet returned?

Malcolm   My liege,
They are not yet come back. But I have spoke
5   With one that saw him die: who did report
That very frankly he confessed his treasons,
Implored your highness' pardon, and set forth
A deep repentance: nothing in his life
Became him like the leaving it; he died
10   As one that had been studied in his death,
To throw away the dearest thing he owed
As 'twere a careless trifle.

Duncan   There's no art
To find the mind's construction in the face:
15   He was a gentleman on whom I built
An absolute trust.

[*Enter* **Macbeth, Banquo, Ross,** *and* **Angus**]

                        O worthiest cousin!
The sin of my ingratitude even now
Was heavy on me. Thou art so far before,
20   That swiftest wing of recompense is slow

King Duncan's palace at Forres. Fanfare of trumpets. **King Duncan, Malcolm, Donalbain,** *and* **Lennox** *enter with their servants.*

Duncan   Has the former thane of Cawdor been executed? Haven't those who were in charge returned yet?

Malcolm   My lord, they have not yet returned. But I have spoken to someone who saw Cawdor die. This man said that he very frankly confessed his treason, begged Your Highness's pardon, and said he was deeply sorry. He did nothing in life as well as the way he died. He died as if he had been practicing how to throw away his life, as if this most precious possession were nothing.

Duncan   There is no way to tell what someone is thinking by studying his face. Cawdor was a gentleman I trusted completely.

[**Macbeth, Banquo, Ross,** *and* **Angus** *enter*]

[*To* **Macbeth**] Oh worthiest cousin! Just now I was feeling very ungrateful. My thanks can't catch up to your actions on my behalf. I wish you had done less, so I might feel that my

To overtake thee. Would thou hadst less deserved,
That the proportion both of thanks and payment
Might have been mine! only I have left to say,
More is thy due than more than all can pay.

25 **Macbeth**   The service and the loyalty I owe,
In doing it, pays itself. Your highness' part
Is to receive our duties: and our duties
Are to your throne and state, children and servants;
Which do but what they should, by doing every thing
30 Safe toward your love and honour.

Duncan   Welcome hither:
I have begun to plant thee, and will labour
To make thee full of growing. Noble Banquo,
That hast no less deserved, nor must be known
35 No less to have done so: let me infold thee,
And hold thee to my heart.

Banquo   There if I grow,
The harvest is your own.

Duncan   My plenteous joys,
40 Wanton in fulness, seek to hide themselves
In drops of sorrow . . . Sons, kinsmen, thanes,
And you whose places are the nearest, know,
We will establish our estate upon
Our eldest, Malcolm, whom we name hereafter
45 The Prince of Cumberland: which honour must
Not unaccompanied invest him only,
But signs of nobleness, like stars, shall shine
On all deservers. From hence to Inverness,
And bind us further to you.

50 **Macbeth**   The rest is labour, which is not used for you:
I'll be myself the harbinger, and make joyful
The hearing of my wife with your approach;
So humbly take my leave.

thanks and rewards could be more generous. As it is, all I can say is that I owe you more than I can pay.

Macbeth Being your loyal servant is payment enough. Your Highness's role is to accept our loyal service. We are like children and servants in our duty to your throne and majesty. When we do everything we can to protect you whom we love and honor, we are only doing what we should.

Duncan Welcome here. My goodwill toward you is well established, and I will make sure you benefit greatly from it. Noble Banquo, you are no less deserving than Macbeth, and everyone must be told of this. Let me embrace you and hold you to my heart.

Banquo If I grow in your favor, the gain will all be yours.

Duncan My great joys are so unrestrained that they make me weep. Sons, kinsmen, thanes, and all those close to me, let it be known that I will leave my kingdom to my eldest son, Malcolm. As heir to the throne, he will now have the title of Prince of Cumberland. This honor to him will be accompanied by rewards to all those who are deserving. From here, we will travel to Macbeth's castle at Inverness, strengthening our bond.

Macbeth When I'm not serving you I get weary. So I'll go ahead as messenger, and give my wife the joyful news of your visit. I humbly take my leave.

Duncan   My worthy Cawdor!

55 **Macbeth**   The Prince of Cumberland! that is a step
       On which I must fall down, or else o'er-leap,
       For in my way it lies. Stars, hide your fires!
       Let not light see my black and deep desires:
       The eye wink at the hand; yet let that be
60   Which the eye fears, when it is done, to see.

                                                    [*Exit*]

    Duncan   True, worthy Banquo; he is full so valiant,
       And in his commendations I am fed:
       It is a banquet to me. Let's after him,
       Whose care is gone before to bid us welcome:
65   It is a peerless kinsman.

                              [*Flourish. Exeunt*]

Duncan My worthy Cawdor!

Macbeth [*to himself*] The Prince of Cumberland! That is a step
that lies in my path. It will trip me up unless I leap over it.
Stars, hide your fires! Don't expose my dark, hidden desires.
Let my eye be blind to what my hand does. But I must do the
thing that my eye fears to see.

[**Macbeth** *exits*]

Duncan It is true, worthy Banquo. Macbeth is fully as brave as
you say. I love to hear you praise him; those praises are like a
feast to me. Let's follow him: He went ahead to prepare a
welcome for us. He has no equal as a kinsman.

[*Fanfare of trumpets. They exit*]

Act I

Scene V

Inverness. Macbeth's castle. Enter **Lady Macbeth,** *reading a letter.*

Lady Macbeth 'They met me in the day of success; and I have
learned by the perfect'st report, they have more in them than
mortal knowledge. When I burned in desire to question them
further, they made themselves air, into which they vanished.
5   Whiles I stood rapt in the wonder of it, came missives from
the king, who all-hailed me, 'Thane of Cawdor', by which
title, before, these Weird Sisters saluted me, and referred me
to the coming on of time, with 'Hail, king that shalt be!' This
have I thought good to deliver thee, my dearest partner of
10   greatness, that thou mightst not lose the due of rejoicing, by
being ignorant of what greatness is promised thee. Lay it to
thy heart, and farewell.'
Glamis thou art, and Cawdor; and shalt be
What thou art promised: yet do I fear thy nature;
15   It is too full o'th' milk of human kindness
To catch the nearest way: thou wouldst be great;
Art not without ambition, but without
The illness should attend it: what thou wouldst highly,
That wouldst thou holily; wouldst not play false,
20   And yet wouldst wrongly win: thou'ldst have, great Glamis,
That which cries 'Thus thou must do', if thou have it,
And that which rather thou dost fear to do
Than wishest should be undone. Hie thee thither,
That I may pour my spirits in thine ear,

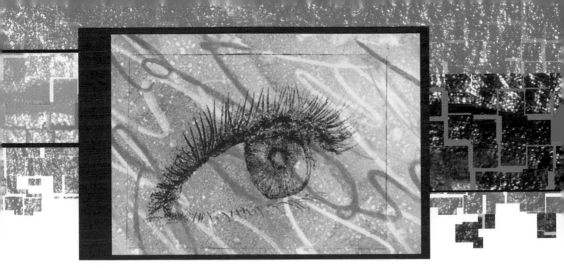

Macbeth's castle at Inverness. **Lady Macbeth** *enters, reading a letter.*

Lady Macbeth [*reading aloud*] "The Weird Sisters met me on the day of our victory. I have been very reliably informed that they have supernatural knowledge. When I was full of desire to question them further, they disappeared into thin air. While I stood amazed, messengers from the King arrived and saluted me as thane of Cawdor. The Weird Sisters had earlier greeted me with the same title, and then they predicted that I would be king. I wanted you to know this, my dearest partner in greatness, so that you would not miss any enjoyment because you were unaware of the greatness promised you. Keep this news secret. Farewell." [*She stops reading and begins to speak her thoughts*] You are thane of Glamis, and of Cawdor, and shall be what you are promised. But I mistrust your nature. You are too soft-hearted to take shortcuts. You wish to be great. You have ambition, but you lack the ruthlessness that should go with it. You want to get power in a moral way. You don't want to cheat, but you want to win unfairly. Great Glamis, you wish for something that requires a necessary act to get it, but you are frightened to do what you would still like to have done. Get here quickly, so I can fill you with my own inspiration. The strength of my

25 And chastise with the valour of my tongue
All that impedes thee from the golden round,
Which fate and metaphysical aid doth seem
To have thee crowned withal.

[*Enter a* **Messenger**]

What is your tiding?

30 **Messenger** The king comes here to-night.

Lady Macbeth   Thou'rt mad to say it!
Is not thy master with him? who, were't so,
Would have informed for preparation.

Messenger So please you, it is true: our thane is coming:
35 One of my fellows had the speed of him;
Who, almost dead for breath, had scarcely more
Than would make up his message.

Lady Macbeth   Give him tending;
He brings great news. [**Messenger** *goes*] The raven himself
40   is hoarse
That croaks the fatal entrance of Duncan
Under my battlements. Come, you spirits
That tend on mortal thoughts, unsex me here,
And fill me from the crown to the toe top-full
45 Of direst cruelty! make thick my blood;
Stop up th'access and passage to remorse,
That no compunctious visitings of nature
Shake my fell purpose, nor keep peace between
The effect and it! Come to my woman's breasts,
50 And take my milk for gall, you murdering ministers,
Wherever in your sightless substances
You wait on nature's mischief! Come, thick night,
And pall thee in the dunnest smoke of hell,
That my keen knife see not the wound it makes,
55 Nor heaven peep through the blanket of the dark,
To cry 'Hold, hold!'

words will overcome the fears that stand between you and the golden crown that fate and magic seem to have promised you.

[*A* **Messenger** *enters*]

What is your news?

Messenger   The King is coming here tonight.

Lady Macbeth   You are mad to say it! Isn't your master with him? If the King were coming, your master would have sent me a message so I could prepare.

Messenger   With respect, it is true. Our thane is coming. One of my fellow messengers just beat him here. The messenger was so exhausted he had only enough breath left to deliver his message.

Lady Macbeth   Look after him; he brings great news.

[*The* **Messenger** *exits*]

The raven, which tells when death is coming, croaks himself hoarse to announce Duncan's fatal arrival at my castle. Come, you spirits that serve deadly thoughts, rid me of my woman's soft nature and fill me from head to foot with the most dreadful cruelty. Make my blood thick. Keep me from feeling pity, so that conscience will not come between my deadly plan and its accomplishment. You agents of murder who lurk unseen and assist evil, make the milk in my breasts bitter! Come, thick night, and cover yourself in the blackest smoke of hell, so that my sharp knife will not see the wound it makes, and heaven won't peep through the blanket of darkness to cry, "Stop, stop!"

[*Enter* **Macbeth**]

                          Great Glamis! worthy Cawdor!
Greater than both, by the all-hail hereafter!
Thy letters have transported me beyond
60   This ignorant present, and I feel now
The future in the instant.

Macbeth   My dearest love,
Duncan comes here to-night.

Lady Macbeth   And when goes hence?

65 **Macbeth** To-morrow, as he purposes.

Lady Macbeth   O, never
Shall sun that morrow see!
Your face, my thane, is as a book where men
May read strange matters. To beguile the time,
70   Look like the time; bear welcome in your eye.
Your hand, your tongue: look like the innocent flower,
But be the serpent under't. He that's coming
Must be provided for: and you shall put
This night's great business into my dispatch,
75   Which shall to all our nights and days to come
Give solely sovereign sway and masterdom.

Macbeth We will speak further.

Lady Macbeth   Only look up clear:
To alter favour ever is to fear:
80   Leave all the rest to me.

                                        [*Exeunt*]

[**Macbeth** *enters*]

Great Glamis! Worthy Cawdor! And a greeting greater than both yet to come! Your letters have carried me beyond the doubtful present, so that I can feel the future here right now.

Macbeth   My dearest love, Duncan is coming here tonight.

Lady Macbeth   And when will he leave?

Macbeth   He plans to leave tomorrow.

Lady Macbeth   Oh, he'll never see that day! My thane, your face is like a book in which men may read strange things. To deceive the rest of the world, look natural. Keep welcome in your eye, your hand, and your tongue. Look like the innocent flower, but be the serpent under it. We must prepare for our guest. You must let me handle tonight's great business, which shall make us supreme in all the nights and days to come.

Macbeth   We must speak further about this.

Lady Macbeth   Just look innocent; a change in your manner will arouse suspicion. Leave all the rest to me.

[**Macbeth** *and* **Lady Macbeth** *exit*]

Act I

Scene VI

Enter **King Duncan, Malcolm, Donalbain, Banquo, Lennox, Macduff, Ross, Angus,** *and* **Attendants.**

Duncan This castle hath a pleasant seat; the air
Nimbly and sweetly recommends itself
Unto our gentle senses.

Banquo   This guest of summer,
5 The temple-haunting martlet, does approve,
By his loved mansionry, that the heaven's breath
Smells wooingly here: no jutty, frieze,
Buttress, nor coign of vantage, but this bird
Hath made his pendent bed and procreant cradle:
10 Where they most breed and haunt, I have observed
The air is delicate.

[*Enter* **Lady Macbeth**]

Duncan   See, see! our honoured hostess!
The love that follows us sometime is our trouble,
Which still we thank as love. Herein I teach you
15 How you shall bid God 'ild us for your pains,
And thank us for your trouble.

King Duncan, Malcolm, Donalbain, Banquo, Lennox, Macduff, Ross, and **Angus** *enter with their servants, arriving at Macbeth's castle.*

Duncan This castle has pleasant surroundings. The air smells fresh and sweet to me.

Banquo The swallows, which usually build their nests in churches during the summer, are nesting everywhere on this castle. That shows that the air is pleasing. I have observed that wherever these birds choose to live and breed, the air is mild.

[**Lady Macbeth** *enters*]

Duncan [*using "we" and "our" to mean "I" and "my," in royal fashion*] Look! Here's our honored hostess! [*To* **Lady Macbeth**] The love of our subjects is sometimes a burden, but we still are thankful for it. I say this to teach you to be thankful for the trouble we cause you, since it shows our love.

Lady Macbeth   All our service
    In every point twice done and then done double,
    Were poor and single business to contend
20   Against those honours deep and broad, wherewith
    Your majesty loads our house: for those of old,
    And the late dignities heaped up to them,
    We rest your hermits.

Duncan   Where's the thane of Cawdor?
25   We coursed him at the heels, and had a purpose
    To be his purveyor: but he rides well,
    And his great love (sharp as his spur) hath holp him
    To his home before us. Fair and noble hostess,
    We are your guest to-night.

30 **Lady Macbeth**   Your servants ever
    Have theirs, themselves, and what is theirs, in compt,
    To make their audit at your highness' pleasure,
    Still to return your own.

Duncan   Give me your hand:
35   Conduct me to mine host; we love him highly,
    And shall continue our graces towards him.
    By your leave, hostess.

                          [*Exeunt*]

Lady Macbeth If every detail of what we do for you were doubled and doubled again, it would still be a small return for all Your Majesty has done for our family. For both past honors and recent rewards you've given us, you'll always be in our thankful prayers.

Duncan Where's the thane of Cawdor? We followed close behind him, hoping to reach here first. But he rides well, and his great love for you, sharp as his spur, has helped him to get home before us. Fair and noble hostess, we are your guest tonight.

Lady Macbeth We are your servants. We hold ourselves, our servants, and all our possessions in trust from you, and are always ready to return them to you.

Duncan Give me your hand. Lead me to our host. We love him greatly, and we shall continue to honor him. [*Offering his hand to* **Lady Macbeth**] With your permission, hostess.

[*They exit*]

Act I

Scene VII

Macbeth's castle. Enter a **sewer** *directing divers servants.*
Then enter **Macbeth.**

Macbeth   If it were done, when 'tis done, then 'twere well
It were done quickly: if th' assassination
Could trammel up the consequence, and catch,
With his surcease, success; that but this blow
5   Might be the be-all and the end-all here,
But here, upon this bank and shoal of time,
We'd jump the life to come. But in these cases
We still have judgement here: that we but teach
Blood instructions, which being taught return
10   To plague th'inventor; this even-handed justice
Commends th'ingredience of our poisoned chalice
To our own lips. He's here in double trust:
First, as I am his kinsman and his subject,
Strong both against the deed: then, as his host,
15   Who should against his murderer shut the door,
Not bear the knife myself. Besides, this Duncan
Hath borne his faculties so meek, hath been
So clear in his great office, that his virtues
Will plead like angels, trumpet-tongued, against
20   The deep damnation of his taking-off;
And pity, like a naked new-born babe,
Striding the blast, or Heaven's cherubin, horsed
Upon the sightless couriers of the air,

Macbeth's castle. A butler and other servants carrying dishes enter. Then **Macbeth** *enters.*

Macbeth   If it could all be over with once the deed was done, then it should be done right away. If the murder would have no consequences and would bring success with his death— so that one blow would end the matter here and now—then we would risk the life to come. But we are usually punished in this life. We teach violent lessons that, once they're taught, return to trouble us. This even-handed justice will result in our drinking the poison that we ourselves placed in a cup. The king should be able to trust me for two reasons. First, because I am his kinsman and his subject—both strong arguments against the deed. Second, because I am his host, who should shut the door against his murderer, not carry the knife myself. Besides, Duncan has ruled so gently and honestly that his virtues will plead against the great evil of his murder as loudly as angels blowing trumpets. Pity, like a naked infant riding the wind or angels mounted on the invisible air,

Shall blow the horrid deed in every eye,
25   That tears shall drown the wind. I have no spur
To prick the sides of my intent, but only
Vaulting ambition, which o'erleaps itself,
And falls on th'other –

[*Enter* **Lady Macbeth**]

                     How now! what news?

30   **Lady Macbeth** He has almost supped; why have you left
the chamber?

Macbeth Hath he asked for me?

Lady Macbeth   Know you not he has?

Macbeth We will proceed no further in this business:
35   He hath honoured me of late, and I have bought
Golden opinions from all sorts of people,
Which would be worn now in their newest gloss,
Not cast aside so soon.

Lady Macbeth   Was the hope drunk
40   Wherein you dressed yourself? hath it slept since?
And wakes it now, to look so green and pale
At what it did so freely? From this time
Such I account thy love. Art thou afeard
To be the same in thine own act and valour
45   As thou art in desire? Wouldst thou have that
Which thou esteem'st the ornament of life,
And live a coward in thine own esteem,
Letting 'I dare not' wait upon 'I would',
Like the poor cat i'th'adage?

50   **Macbeth**   Prithee, peace:
I dare do all that may become a man;
Who dares do more is none.

shall blow the horrible deed into every eye, so that tears shall fall like rain. I have nothing to spur me on in this plan except ambition, which can leap so high that it misses its goal, leading to a fall—

[**Lady Macbeth** *enters*]

Well? What is the news?

Lady Macbeth   He is almost finished eating. Why have you left the room?

Macbeth   Has he asked for me?

Lady Macbeth   Don't you know that he has?

Macbeth   We will go no further with this plan. He has honored me recently, and I have won admiration from many people. These things should be enjoyed while they're new, not thrown away so soon.

Lady Macbeth   Was your former ambition just drunk? Has it been sleeping? And now does it wake up sick at the thought of what it did when it was drunk? From now on, I'll know what your love is worth. Are you afraid to be as brave in your actions as you are in your desires? Can you have what you value as life's greatest prize, the crown, and be a coward at heart? Will you let "I dare not" always follow "I would," like the poor cat in the proverb?

Macbeth   Please, peace! I dare do all that a man should do. Who dares do more is not human.

Lady Macbeth   What beast was't then
That made you break this enterprise to me?
55 When you durst do it, then you were a man;
And, to be more than what you were, you would
Be so much more the man. Nor time nor place
Did then adhere, and yet you would make both:
They have made themselves, and that their fitness now
60 Does unmake you. I have given suck, and know
How tender 'tis to love the babe that milks me –
I would, while it was smiling in my face,
Have plucked my nipple from his boneless gums,
And dashed the brains out, had I so sworn as you
65 Have done to this.

Macbeth   If we should fail?

Lady Macbeth   We fail?
But screw your courage to the sticking place,
And we'll not fail. When Duncan is asleep –
70 Whereto the rather shall his day's hard journey
Soundly invite him – his two chamberlains
Will I with wine and wassail so convince,
That memory, the warder of the brain,
Shall be a fume, and the receipt of reason
75 A limbec only: when in swinish sleep
Their drenched natures lie as in a death,
What cannot you and I perform upon
Th'unguarded Duncan? what not put upon
His spongy officers, shall bear the guilt
80 Of our great quell?

Macbeth   Bring forth men-children only!
For thy undaunted mettle should compose
Nothing but males. Will it not be received,
When we have marked with blood those sleepy two
85 Of his own chamber, and used their very daggers,
That they have done't?

Lady Macbeth What beast was it then that made you tell me about this plan? You were a man when you dared to do it. You would be even more of a man if you still had ambition. Neither the time nor place presented themselves then, but still you were ready to make the time and place. Now that they have made themselves, your courage is gone. I have nursed and know how tender it is to love the child at my breast. While my child was smiling up at me, I would have plucked my nipple from his toothless mouth and dashed his brains out if I had sworn to do it, as you have sworn to do this.

Macbeth But if we should fail?

Lady Macbeth We fail? Just screw your courage to its readiest point and we won't fail. When Duncan is asleep—and his hard day's journey will make him sleep soundly—I'll get the two attendants of his bedchamber so drunk that they'll remember nothing, their minds will be so befuddled. When they're sleeping like pigs and dead to the world, what can't you and I do to the unguarded Duncan? We can accuse his drunken officers, who shall get the blame for our great murder.

Macbeth Have male children only! Your courageous spirit should produce nothing but males. When we have smeared the sleepy attendants of his bedchamber with blood, and used their own daggers, won't everyone believe they have done it?

Lady Macbeth   Who dares receive it other,
As we shall make our griefs and clamour roar
Upon his death?

90 **Macbeth**   I am settled, and bend up
Each corporal agent to this terrible feat.
Away, and mock the time with fairest show:
False face must hide what the false heart doth know.

[Exeunt]

Lady Macbeth   Who would dare to believe otherwise, since we shall wail so loudly at his death?

Macbeth   I am ready. I will strain every muscle to this terrible deed. Let's go and deceive the world with pleasant looks. A false face must hide what the false heart knows.

[**Macbeth** *and* **Lady Macbeth** *exit*]

Comprehension   Check What You Know

1. What two enemies does the kingdom of Scotland face? How are they overcome?

2. What powers do the Three Witches seem to possess? What do they predict will happen to Macbeth and Banquo?

3. What kind of ruler does Duncan appear to be?

4. How do Macbeth and Banquo differ in their reactions to the Witches' predictions and the news of Macbeth's new title? What does this suggest about their characters?

5. How does Macbeth react to Duncan's naming of his son Malcolm as his heir?

6. After reading her husband's letter, what does Lady Macbeth say about him?

7. What does Lady Macbeth's reaction to the news of Duncan's visit show about her nature?

8. What is ironic, or "off," about Duncan's first impression when he arrives at Macbeth's castle?

9. Why does Macbeth tell his wife that she should have only male children?

Activities & Role-Playing   Classes or Informal Groups

Mirror, Mirror How do you picture Lady Macbeth? Is she young or middle-aged? Fair or dark? Seductive or stern? How does she dress and wear her hair? Does she like jewelry? Create a portrait of Lady Macbeth. You may draw or paint a picture, or you may write an essay that describes her.

Bubble, Bubble, Toil and Trouble Witches are serious business in *Macbeth*. They stir their cauldron, cast spells, and when they speak to Macbeth, they tell the truth about the future—sort of—in confusing riddles and chants.

©Evening Standard/Hulton/Archive

Join up with four others and discuss how you would perform Scene 3. Then divide up the roles and read aloud the confrontation between the Witches and Macbeth and Banquo (lines 1–80). Remember that the Witches must be believable and threatening and that Macbeth and Banquo take them seriously.

Discussion   Classes or Informal Groups

1. Discuss Macbeth's values as they are revealed in Act 1. What seems to influence his behavior most? Religion? Ethics? Self-interest? Emotional drives?

2. Would Macbeth have decided to kill the King without the Witches' prophecy? Discuss how his encounter with the Witches affects his decision.

3. Some critics say that Macbeth and his wife may be the happiest married couple in all of Shakespeare's plays. Do you agree? How do Macbeth and his wife deal with one another? Who seems to be the dominant partner?

Suggestions for Writing   Improve Your Skills

1. "Fair is foul, and foul is fair," chant the Witches in Scene 1. As Macbeth and Banquo near the Witches, Macbeth says, "So foul and fair a day I have not seen" (1, 3, 39). He is saying that the day is fair because the battles have gone his way, but the day is foul because of the weather. Statements like this— where opposite statements are true—are called *paradoxes.*

   Make a list of things that happen in Act 1 that show that "foul is fair, and fair is foul." Consider when people say that an event or act is wonderful, when actually something bad could come of it. Then write a paragraph about the effect that such paradoxes have on the mood of the play.

2. Shakespeare had no way to present a battle on stage. There just was not enough room. Read the descriptions of the battles of the day. Then pretend that you were one of the soldiers that fought against the Thane of Cawdor and the general from Norway. Write a diary entry describing the events of the battle. You may be fighting for or against Duncan's forces.

3. Everyone in Act 1 has a "picture" of Macbeth—he is a fearless soldier; he is a fierce defender of the King; he may believe what the Witches say. Macbeth himself reveals that he is willing to consider more than one possibility in a situation and that he wants to be king. Lady Macbeth, however, thinks that Macbeth is too soft. Pretend that you are a newspaper reporter who interviewed Macbeth and others who know him well. Then write two or three paragraphs for a "personality piece" describing this Man of the Moment.

All the World's a Stage Introduction

When night falls, some predators hunt! When he enters Macbeth's castle, King Duncan may be walking into a trap. After all, Macbeth thinks he's got a good shot at becoming Scotland's king. But Macbeth knows that to do this he might have to break a "double trust." Since he is Duncan's kinsman and subject, killing the king will make him a traitor. On top of that, Duncan is Macbeth's guest. A host was responsible for the safety of someone under his roof. In the violent society of *Macbeth,* this trust between a guest and his host (or hostess) would have been almost sacred.

It seems that evil deeds are planned inside Macbeth's castle walls. And as the power struggles get worse inside, bizarre events also occur outdoors. Act 2 contains reports of some very strange goings-on in the natural world.

What's in a Name? Characters

There's only one comic figure in *Macbeth,* the drunken Porter. He provides comic relief while discussing some quite serious things. And when he imagines he's the gatekeeper of hell, he's not that far off. Macbeth's home is a frightening place.

Meanwhile, life under Macbeth's roof is no laughing matter for Malcolm and Donalbain, King Duncan's two sons. Duncan has already named Malcolm as heir to his throne. That's bad news for Macbeth, who can't "succeed" to the throne with Malcolm and Donalbain in his way.

Banquo also has a son, Fleance. We'll meet him in Act 2. We'll also meet Macduff, another of the Scottish nobles. Though "Macduff" sounds a little like "Macbeth," these two characters will turn out to be quite different.

COME WHAT MAY Things to Watch For

Macbeth may be a very dark play, but one color stands out—red. By the end of Act 2, you may feel as if Shakespeare had smeared his characters with this color. Watch for how images of smearing and staining start to fill Shakespeare's play. Meanwhile, the Macbeths try to paint their own picture of innocence and guilt. How well do they fool their guests?

Macbeth is full of elemental, primal sights and sounds—colors, noises, and animals that seem to be right under our eyes, ears, and noses. Act 2's "sound-track" is full of sudden, scary noises. Pay attention to how Shakespeare uses these sounds to build suspense and to show us the mood of the host couple.

All Our Yesterdays Historical and Social Context

Shakespeare probably wrote *Macbeth* around 1606. England was reeling at that time with news of a plot to kill its king, James I. The plot stemmed from religious conflict. James was a Protestant and ruled England as a Protestant nation. Catholics faced harsh discrimination. In November 1605, a group of Catholic conspirators carried out the "Gunpowder Plot." They smuggled kegs of gunpowder to an area beneath the Parliament building. The goal was to blow up both houses of Parliament (the English government) while the king was there, destroying the entire government. Had the plot succeeded, it would have been as if someone had blown up the president, vice-president, both houses of Congress, and the Supreme Court, all at the same time.

One of the people tried for treason was a Jesuit priest, Henry Garnet. He used what the defense called "equivocation." It said that a lie was not a lie if the speaker had in mind a different meaning that made the statement true. It was a way to mislead your questioners while keeping a clear conscience.

The Play's the Thing Staging

Act 2 contains lots of movement. People are coming in and out of the castle and also moving around a great deal inside. How did Shakespeare's audience keep track of all this? It's possible that the actors used the doors in the back of the stage so that the "front door" of the castle was always the same door on the stage. If an actor entered through this door, you knew his character was coming from "outside." If he entered through a different door, you knew he was coming from somewhere inside the castle.

The stage might also have been set up to show an exterior and interior. The main acting area of the Globe is sometimes called the Platform. At the back of it was a curtained area used to show "rooms" for some interior scenes. In Act 2, Scenes 1 and 4, which are set in the courtyard of Macbeth's castle, may have been played on the Platform alone. Scenes 2 and 3, which involve movement from one area of the castle to another, may have been played on the Platform and in this curtained alcove or "room."

My Words Fly Up Language

During the first scene of Act 2, Macbeth mentions a goddess named Hecate. It's not the last time this demanding lady will show up in the play! In Greek mythology, Hecate is a goddess of the dead and a friend to witches. She is called "pale Hecate" because she is linked with the moon. Dogs, honey, and black lambs were sacrificed to her at crossroads.

Another sinister figure is mentioned in Act 2. In the Bible's Old Testament, Beelzebub ("Lord of the Flies") was a pagan god. Later, he became known as a ruler of demons. When the Porter imagines he's letting Beelzebub in at Macbeth's door, he's opening the door to some very bad company!

Act II

Scene I

Macbeth's castle, a few hours later. Enter **Banquo,** *and*
Fleance *with a torch before him.*

Banquo   How goes the night, boy?

Fleance   The moon is down;
I have not heard the clock.

Banquo   And she goes down at twelve.

5   **Fleance**   I take't, 'tis later, sir.

Banquo   Hold, take my sword. There's husbandry in heaven,
Their candles are all out. Take thee that too.
A heavy summons lies like lead upon me,
And yet I would not sleep. Merciful powers,
10   Restrain in me the cursed thoughts that nature
Gives way to in repose! Give me my sword.
Who's there?

[*Enter* **Macbeth,** *and a* **Servant** *with a torch.*]

Macbeth   A friend.

Banquo   What, sir, not yet at rest? The king's a-bed.
15   He hath been in unusual pleasure, and
Sent forth great largess to your offices.
This diamond he greets your wife withal,
By the name of most kind hostess; and shut up
In measureless content.

Macbeth's castle, a few hours later. **Banquo** *enters with* **Fleance**, *who is carrying a torch.*

Banquo What time is it, boy?

Fleance The moon is down. I have not heard the clock.

Banquo The moon goes down at midnight.

Fleance It must be later then, sir.

Banquo Here, take my sword. They practice economy in heaven. The lights are all out. Take this, too. [*He gives him his belt and dagger*] I feel as heavy as lead, and yet I don't want to go to sleep. Good angels, keep away the evil dreams that come to me with rest. [*He hears a noise*] Give me my sword. Who's there? [*He takes his sword*]

[**Macbeth** *enters, accompanied by his* **Servant** *carrying a torch*]

Macbeth A friend.

Banquo What, sir? You're not in bed yet? The King has gone to bed. He has been unusually happy and has sent large gifts to your household. He means to give your wife this diamond for being such a kind hostess. He went to bed highly contented.

20 **Macbeth**   Being unprepared,
    Our will became the servant to defect,
    Which else should free have wrought.

Banquo   All's well.
    I dreamt last night of the three Weird Sisters:
25 To you they have showed some truth.

Macbeth   I think not of them:
    Yet, when we can entreat an hour to serve,
    We would spend it in some words upon that business,
    If you would grant the time.

30 **Banquo**   At your kind'st leisure.

Macbeth If you shall cleave to my consent, when 'tis,
    It shall make honour for you.

Banquo   So I lose none
    In seeking to augment it, but still keep
35 My bosom franchised and allegiance clear,
    I shall be counselled.

Macbeth   Good repose the while!

Banquo Thanks, sir: the like to you!

                    [*Exeunt* **Banquo** *and* **Fleance**]

Macbeth Go bid thy mistress, when my drink is ready,
40 She strike upon the bell. Get thee to bed.

                            [*Exit* **Servant**]

    Is this a dagger which I see before me,
    The handle toward my hand? Come, let me clutch thee.
    I have thee not, and yet I see thee still.
    Art thou not, fatal vision, sensible
45 To feeling as to sight? or art thou but

Macbeth We weren't expecting him, so we weren't able to entertain him as well as we would have liked.

Banquo You did very well. I dreamed about the Weird Sisters last night. Some of what they told you has come true.

Macbeth I don't think about them. Yet, when I can find the time, I would like to speak of that business with you, if you can spare a moment.

Banquo I'm ready whenever you're free.

Macbeth If you give me your support at the right moment, you shall benefit.

Banquo So long as I don't lose my honor in trying to gain more, and remain free from guilt and loyal to the King, I'm ready to take your advice.

Macbeth Meanwhile, sleep well!

Banquo Thanks, sir. The same to you.

[**Banquo** *and* **Fleance** *exit*]

Macbeth [*to his* **Servant**] Go tell your mistress to ring the bell when my drink is ready. Then go to bed.

[*The* **Servant** *exits.* **Macbeth** *looks into space as if he saw something there*]

Is this a dagger that I see in front of me, with its handle turned toward my hand? Come, let me clutch you. I cannot grasp you, yet I still see you. Can't I touch you, deadly sight,

A dagger of the mind, a false creation,
Proceeding from the heat-oppressed brain?
I see thee yet, in form as palpable
As this which now I draw.
50 Thou marshall'st me the way that I was going,
And such an instrument I was to use!
Mine eyes are made the fools o'th'other senses,
Or else worth all the rest: I see thee still;
And on thy blade and dudgeon gouts of blood,
55 Which was not so before. There's no such thing:
It is the bloody business which informs
Thus to mine eyes. Now o'er the one half-world
Nature seems dead, and wicked dreams abuse
The curtained sleep; now witchcraft celebrates
60 Pale Hecate's off'rings; and withered Murder,
Alarumed by his sentinel, the wolf,
Whose howl's his watch, thus with his stealthy pace,
With Tarquin's ravishing strides, towards his design
Moves like a ghost. Thou sure and firm-set earth,
65 Hear not my steps, which way they walk, for fear
Thy very stones prate of my whereabout,
And take the present horror from the time,
Which now suits with it. Whiles I threat, he lives:
Words to the heat of deeds too cold breath gives.

[A bell rings]

70 I go, and it is done: the bell invites me.
Hear it not, Duncan, for it is a knell
That summons thee to heaven, or to hell.

[Exit]

as well as see you? Or are you only a dagger of the mind, like a vision produced by a fever? I still see you, as clear in form as this dagger that I pull out now. [*He pulls out his dagger*] You guide me toward where I was going and are the same weapon I was planning to use! Either my eyes are being fooled by my other senses, or else they're the only sense that I can trust. I still see you, and on your blade and handle are smears of blood that were not there before. There's nothing here. It is the bloody business that makes me see this. Now, Nature seems dead throughout half the world. Wicked dreams deceive those who sleep. Now, witches sacrifice to the goddess of the night. Withered Murder is wakened by the howls of his watchdog, the wolf, and moves silently and fiercely toward his victim. You sure and solid earth, don't listen to my steps, so their sound on the stones doesn't show where I'm going or break the dreadful silence that suits my deed. While I rave this way, he goes on living. Words cool the heat of action.

[*A bell rings*]

I go, and it is done. The bell invites me. Do not hear it, Duncan, for it's a bell that summons you to heaven or to hell.

[**Macbeth** *exits*]

Act II

Scene II

Lady Macbeth *enters.*

Lady Macbeth That which hath made them drunk hath made
    me bold:
What hath quenched them hath given me fire. Hark! Peace!
It was the owl that shrieked, the fatal bellman,
5   Which gives the stern'st good-night. He is about it:
The doors are open; and the surfeited grooms
Do mock their charge with snores: I have drugged their
    possetts,
That death and nature do contend about them,
10   Whether they live or die.

Macbeth   Who's there? what, ho!

Lady Macbeth Alack! I am afraid they have awaked,
And 'tis not done: th'attempt and not the deed
Confounds us. Hark! I laid their daggers ready,
15   He could not miss 'em. Had he not resembled
My father as he slept, I had done't.

[*Enter* **Macbeth**]

                         My husband!

Macbeth I have done the deed. Didst thou not hear a noise?

Lady Macbeth I heard the owl scream, and the crickets cry.
20   Did you not speak?

Lady Macbeth *enters.*

Lady Macbeth The wine that has made them drunk has made me bold. What has quenched them has made me fiery. Listen! Quiet! It was the owl that screeched, the deadly watchman that bids good night to those near death. My husband's doing it now. The doors are open, and the drunken servants make a joke of their duty by snoring. I have so drugged their drinks that it's a question whether they will live or die.

Macbeth [*offstage*] Who's there? What's happening?

Lady Macbeth Oh no! I fear they have awakened, and it's not done. The mere attempt, rather than the deed, defeats us. Listen! I laid their daggers ready. He could not miss them. I would have done it myself, if Duncan hadn't looked like my father in his sleep.

[**Macbeth** *enters*]

My husband!

Macbeth I have done the deed. Didn't you hear a noise?

Lady Macbeth I heard the owl scream and the crickets cry. Didn't you speak?

Macbeth When?

Lady Macbeth Now.

Macbeth As I descended?

Lady Macbeth Ay.

25 **Macbeth** Hark!
Who lies i'th' second chamber?

Lady Macbeth Donalbain.

Macbeth This is a sorry sight.

Lady Macbeth A foolish thought, to say a sorry sight.

30 **Macbeth** There's one did laugh in's sleep, and one cried
'Murder!'
That they did wake each other: I stood and heard them:
But they did say their prayers, and addressed them
Again to sleep.

35 **Lady Macbeth** There are two lodged together.

Macbeth One cried 'God bless us!' and 'Amen' the other,
As they had seen me with these hangman's hands:
List'ning their fear, I could not say 'Amen',
When they did say 'God bless us'.

40 **Lady Macbeth** Consider it not so deeply.

Macbeth But wherefore could not I pronounce 'Amen'?
I had most need of blessing, and 'Amen'
Stuck in my throat.

Lady Macbeth These deeds must not be thought
45 After these ways; so, it will make us mad.

Macbeth Methought I heard a voice cry 'Sleep no more!
Macbeth does murder sleep', the innocent sleep,
Sleep that knits up the ravelled sleave of care,
The death of each day's life, sore labour's bath,
50 Balm of hurt minds, great Nature's second course,
Chief nourisher in life's feast, –

Macbeth When?

Lady Macbeth Now.

Macbeth When I came down?

Lady Macbeth Yes.

Macbeth Listen! Who's sleeping in the second bedroom?

Lady Macbeth Donalbain.

Macbeth [*looking at his hands*] This is a sorry sight.

Lady Macbeth It's foolish to say, "a sorry sight."

Macbeth One of them laughed in his sleep, and the other cried, "Murder!" So they woke each other up. I stood and heard them. But they said their prayers and went back to sleep.

Lady Macbeth Two are staying in that room—Malcolm and Donalbain.

Macbeth One cried, "God bless us," and the other answered, "Amen." It was as if they had seen me with these bloody hands. Hearing their fear, I could not say, "Amen," when they said, "God bless us."

Lady Macbeth Don't think about it so much.

Macbeth But why couldn't I say, "Amen"? I had the greatest need of blessing, but "Amen" stuck in my throat.

Lady Macbeth We can't think like this about what we've done. It will make us mad.

Macbeth I thought I heard a voice cry, "Sleep no more! Macbeth has murdered sleep." Innocent sleep, sleep that untangles the knots of our worries, the goal of each day, a soothing rest from work, healing for sick minds, Nature's reviving course, the main course in life's feast—

Lady Macbeth   What do you mean?

Macbeth   Still it cried 'Sleep no more!' to all the house:
  'Glamis hath murdered sleep, and therefore Cawdor
55 Shall sleep no more: Macbeth shall sleep no more!'

Lady Macbeth   Who was it that thus cried? Why,
      worthy thane,
  You do unbend your noble strength, to think
  So brainsickly of things. Go get some water,
60 And wash this filthy witness from your hand.
  Why did you bring these daggers from the place?
  They must lie there: go carry them, and smear
  The sleepy grooms with blood.

Macbeth   I'll go no more:
65 I am afraid to think what I have done;
  Look on't again I dare not.

Lady Macbeth   Infirm of purpose!
  Give me the daggers: the sleeping and the dead
  Are but as pictures: 'tis the eye of childhood
70 That fears a painted devil. If he do bleed,
  I'll gild the faces of the grooms withal,
  For it must seem their guilt.

                    [*She exits. Knocking within*]

Macbeth   Whence is that knocking?
  How is't with me, when every noise appals me?
75 What hands are here? ha! they pluck out mine eyes!
  Will all great Neptune's ocean wash this blood
  Clean from my hand? No; this my hand will rather
  The multitudinous seas incarnadine,
  Making the green one red.

  [**Lady Macbeth** *returns*]

Lady Macbeth What do you mean?

Macbeth Still it cried, "Sleep no more!" to the whole house. "Glamis has murdered sleep, and therefore Cawdor shall sleep no more. Macbeth shall sleep no more!"

Lady Macbeth Who was it that cried like that? Why, you will let your noble strength go slack, my lord, if you think of things so insanely. Go get some water, and wash this telltale mess from your hands. Why did you bring these daggers from the place? They must remain there. Go, take them, and smear the sleepy servants with blood.

Macbeth I won't go back. I am afraid to think of what I've done. I don't dare look at it again.

Lady Macbeth Weakling! Give me the daggers. Sleeping and dead people are like pictures. Only a child fears a picture— even of a devil. If Duncan's still bleeding, I'll color the faces of the servants with his blood, for it must appear they did it.

[**Lady Macbeth** *exits. There is a sound of knocking*]

Macbeth Where is that knocking coming from? What is happening to me when every noise terrifies me? Whose hands are these? Ha! They pluck out my eyes! Would all the water in the great sea god's ocean wash this blood clean from my hand? No, my hand would instead turn the many seas bloody, making their green waters all red.

[**Lady Macbeth** *returns*]

80 **Lady Macbeth**   My hands are of your colour; but I shame
To wear a heart so white. [*Knocking*] I hear a knocking
At the south entry: retire we to our chamber:
A little water clears us of this deed:
How easy is it then! Your constancy
85 Hath left you unattended. [*Knocking*] Hark! more knocking.
Get on your nightgown, lest occasion call us
And show us to be watchers: be not lost
So poorly in your thoughts.

Macbeth   To know my deed, 'twere best not know myself.

[*Knocking*]

90 Wake Duncan with thy knocking! I would thou couldst!

[*Exeunt*]

Lady Macbeth My hands are now the same color as yours, but I would be ashamed if my heart were as white. [*Knocking*] I hear a knocking at the south gate. Let's return to our bedroom. A little water will clean up the evidence of our deed. How easy it will be then! Your firmness has deserted you. [*Knocking*] More knocking. Put your robe on, so that if we are called, we won't seem to have been up. Don't get lost in depressing thoughts.

Macbeth I'd rather forget myself than see what I've done. [*Knocking*] Wake Duncan with your knocking! I wish you could!

[**Macbeth** *and* **Lady Macbeth** *exit*]

Act II

Scene III

Knocking within. Enter a **Porter.**

Porter Here's a knocking indeed! If a man were porter of
hell-gate, he should have old turning the key. [*Knocking*]
Knock, knock, knock! Who's there, i'th' name of Beelzebub?
Here's a farmer, that hanged himself on th'expectation of
5   plenty: come in, time-server; have napkins enow about you;
here you'll sweat for't. [*Knocking*] Knock, knock! Who's
there, in th'other devil's name? Faith, here's an equivocator,
that could swear in both the scales against either scale, who
committed treason enough for God's sake, yet could not
10   equivocate to heaven: O, come in, equivocator. [*Knocking*]
Knock, knock, knock! Who's there? Faith, here's an English
tailor come hither, for stealing out of a French hose: come in,
tailor, here you may roast your goose. [*Knocking*] Knock,
knock! never at quiet! What are you? But this place is too cold
15   for hell. I'll devil-porter it no further: I had thought to have
let in some of all professions, that go the primrose way to
th'everlasting bonfire. [*Knocking*] Anon, anon! I pray you,
remember the porter. [*Opens the gate*]

[*Enter* **Macduff** *and* **Lennox**]

Macduff Was it so late, friend, ere you went to bed,
20   That you do lie so late?

Porter Faith, sir, we were carousing till the second cock: and
drink, sir, is a great provoker of three things.

Knocking offstage. A **Porter** *enters.*

Porter Here's a lot of knocking! If a man were the porter at the
gate of hell, he would spend plenty of time turning the key.
[*Knocking*] Knock, knock, knock! Who's there, in the devil's
name? Maybe it's a greedy farmer who hanged himself when
prices fell. Come right in! Bring plenty of handkerchiefs; you'll
sweat a lot here. [*Knocking*] Knock, knock! Who's there, in the
other devil's name? By my faith, here's a false priest, who
would argue that two opposite things were true, and commit
treason in the name of God, but could not swear his way into
heaven. Oh, come in, two-faced! [*Knocking*] Knock, knock,
knock! Who's there? By my faith, here's an English tailor come
here because he kept stealing cloth even when pants got tight.
Come in, tailor. You can heat up your iron here. [*Knocking*]
Knock, knock! No rest! Who are you? But this place is too cold
for hell. I won't be the devil's porter any longer. I imagined I
would be letting in some of all the professions that take the
flowery path to the everlasting bonfire. [*Knocking*] Right away,
right away! [*He opens the gate*] Please, remember the porter.

[**Macduff** *and* **Lennox** *enter*]

Macduff Was it so late before you went to bed, friend, that
you overslept?

Porter By my faith, sir, we were drinking until 3 A.M. And
drink, sir, is a great maker of three things.

Macduff   What three things does drink especially provoke?

Porter   Marry, sir, nose-painting, sleep, and urine. Lechery,
25   sir, it provokes and unprovokes: it provokes the desire, but it
       takes away the performance. Therefore, much drink may be
       said to be an equivocator with lechery: it makes him, and it
       mars him; it sets him on, and it takes him off; it persuades
       him, and disheartens him; makes him stand to, and not stand
30   to: in conclusion, equivocates him in a sleep, and giving him
       the lie, leaves him.

Macduff   I believe drink gave thee the lie last night.

Porter   That it did, sir, i'the very throat on me: but I requited
       him for his lie, and, I think, being too strong for him, though
35   he took up my legs sometime, yet I made a shift to cast him.

Macduff   Is thy master stirring?

[*Enter* **Macbeth**]

Our knocking has awaked him; here he comes.

Lennox   Good-morrow, noble sir.

Macbeth   Good-morrow, both.

40 **Macduff**   Is the king stirring, worthy thane?

Macbeth   Not yet.

Macduff   He did command me to call timely on him;
       I have almost slipped the hour.

Macbeth   I'll bring you to him.

45 **Macduff**   I know this is a joyful trouble to you;
       But yet 'tis one.

Macbeth   The labour we delight in physics pain.
       This is the door.

Macduff   What three things does drink especially make?

Porter   By our lady, sir, it makes red noses, sleep, and urine. Lechery, sir, it makes and then *un*makes. Drink produces the desire, but it takes away the deed. Therefore, a lot of drinking may be said to be two-faced about lechery. It helps it and hurts it. It gets a man started, then stops him. It warms him up and cools him off. It makes him stand ready, then not stand ready. In the end, lechery lies to him in dreams, and calling him a liar, leaves him lying.

Macduff   I think drink left *you* lying last night.

Porter   That it did, sir. Drink got me by the throat. But I got back at it. I was too strong for it. It got me by the legs at times, but finally I threw it up.

Macduff   Is your master awake?

[**Macbeth** *enters*]

Our knocking has awakened him. Here he comes.

Lennox   Good morning, noble sir.

Macbeth   Good morning to you both.

Macduff   Is the King awake, noble thane?

Macbeth   Not yet.

Macduff   He commanded me to call him early. I am almost late.

Macbeth   I'll bring you to him.

Macduff   I know you welcome taking this trouble, but it is trouble.

Macbeth   A labor we delight in is no trouble. This is the door.

Macduff   I'll make so bold to call,
50   For 'tis my limited service.

                                        [*Exit*]

Lennox Goes the king hence to-day?

Macbeth He does: he did appoint so.

Lennox The night has been unruly: where we lay,
        Our chimneys were blown down, and, as they say,
55   Lamentings heard i'th'air, strange screams of death,
        And prophesying with accents terrible
        Of dire combustion and confused events
        New hatched to th'woeful time. The obscure bird
        Clamoured the livelong night: some say, the earth
60   Was feverous and did shake.

Macbeth   'Twas a rough night.

Lennox My young remembrance cannot parallel
        A fellow to it.

        [*Enter* **Macduff**]

Macduff O horror! horror! horror! Tongue, nor heart,
65   Cannot conceive nor name thee!

Macbeth, Lennox   What's the matter?

Macduff Confusion now hath made his masterpiece!
        Most sacrilegious murder hath broke ope
        The Lord's anointed temple, and stole thence
70   The life o'th'building.

Macbeth   What is't you say? the life?

Lennox Mean you his majesty?

Macduff I'll be bold and call him, for it is my appointed task.

[**Macduff** *exits*]

Lennox Does the King leave here today?

Macbeth He does. That was his plan.

Lennox Last night was very stormy. Where we stayed, the chimneys were blown over. People said that they heard cries in the wind, strange screams of death, terrifying predictions of fearful riots and disorders to which the sad times would give birth. An owl screeched all night long. Some people said that the earth was restless and shook.

Macbeth It was a rough night.

Lennox In my short lifetime, I can't remember another like it.

[**Macduff** *enters*]

Macduff O horror! horror! horror! No tongue can speak it, nor heart grasp it!

Macbeth and Lennox [*together*] What's the matter?

Macduff Destruction has triumphed! Unholy murder has invaded the Lord's temple and stolen the life out of the building.

Macbeth What are you saying? "The life"?

Lennox Do you mean His Majesty?

Macduff   Approach the chamber, and destroy your sight
With a new Gorgon: do not bid me speak;
75   See, and then speak yourselves.

[*Exeunt* **Macbeth** *and* **Lennox**]

Awake! awake!
Ring the alarum bell! Murder and treason!
Banquo and Donalbain! Malcolm! awake!
Shake off this downy sleep, death's counterfeit,
80   And look on death itself! up, up, and see
The great doom's image! Malcolm! Banquo!
As from your graves rise up, and walk like sprites,
To countenance this horror! Ring the bell.   [*Bell rings*]

[*Enter* **Lady Macbeth**]

Lady Macbeth   What's the business,
85   That such a hideous trumpet calls to parley
The sleepers of the house? speak, speak!

Macduff   O, gentle lady,
'Tis not for you to hear what I can speak:
The repetition, in a woman's ear,
90   Would murder as it fell.

[*Enter* **Banquo**]

O, Banquo! Banquo!
Our royal master's murdered!

Lady Macbeth   Woe, alas!
What, in our house?

95   **Banquo**   Too cruel, any where.
Dear Duff, I prithee, contradict thyself,
And say it is not so.

Macduff Go to his bedroom and destroy your sight with a horror that will turn you to stone. Do not ask me to speak. Go see, and then speak for yourselves.

[**Macbeth** *and* **Lennox** *exit*]

Awake! awake! Ring the alarm bell! Murder and treason! Banquo and Donalbain! Malcolm! awake! Shake off soft sleep, which mimics death, and look on death itself! Up, up, and get a glimpse of doomsday! Malcolm! Banquo! Rise like the dead from their graves, and walk like ghosts to face this horror! Ring the bell. [*Bell rings*]

[**Lady Macbeth** *enters*]

Lady Macbeth What's going on, that such a fearful noise summons the sleepers of this house to meet? Speak, speak!

Macduff Oh, gentle lady, it is not right for you to hear my words. To repeat them in a woman's ear would kill her as she heard it.

[**Banquo** *enters*]

O Banquo! Banquo! Our royal master's murdered!

Lady Macbeth No! no! What? In our house?

Banquo Too cruel an event anywhere. Dear Duff, I beg you, contradict yourself, and say this isn't so.

[**Macbeth** *and* **Lennox** *return*]

Macbeth Had I but died an hour before this chance,
I had lived a blessed time; for from this instant
100 There's nothing serious in mortality
All is but toys: renown and grace is dead,
The wine of life is drawn, and the mere lees
Is left this vault to brag of.

[*Enter* **Malcolm** *and* **Donalbain**]

Donalbain What is amiss?

105 **Macbeth**   You are, and do not know't:
The spring, the head, the fountain of your blood
Is stopped – the very source of it is stopped.

Macduff Your royal father's murdered.

Malcolm   O, by whom?

110 **Lennox** Those of his chamber, as it seemed, had done't:
Their hands and faces were all badged with blood,
So were their daggers, which unwiped we found
Upon their pillows:
They stared and were distracted, no man's life
115 Was to be trusted with them.

Macbeth O, yet I do repent me of my fury,
That I did kill them.

Macduff   Wherefore did you so?

Macbeth Who can be wise, amazed, temp'rate and furious,
120 Loyal and neutral, in a moment? no man:
Th'expedition of my violent love
Outrun the pauser, reason. Here lay Duncan,
His silver skin laced with his golden blood,
And his gashed stabs looked like a breach in nature
125 For ruin's wasteful entrance: there, the murderers,

[**Macbeth** *and* **Lennox** *return*]

Macbeth   Had I only died an hour before this happened, I would have had a blessed life. For from this instant there's nothing valuable in this world. Everything seems worthless. Fame and honor are dead. The wine of life is gone. Nothing but the bitter dregs remain.

[**Malcolm** *and* **Donalbain** *enter*]

Donalbain   What's the trouble?

Macbeth   Yours, but you don't know it. The spring from which your blood flows—the source, the fountainhead—has been stopped up.

Macduff   Your royal father is murdered.

Malcolm   Oh no! By whom?

Lennox   It appears that his servants did it. Their hands and faces were all stained with blood. So were their daggers. We found the weapons, still not wiped clean, on their pillows. They stared and looked confused. No man's life was safe with them.

Macbeth   Oh, still I regret that in my fury, I killed them.

Macduff   Why *did* you?

Macbeth   Who can be wise and stunned, calm and furious, loyal and neutral, all at the same time? No one. The haste of my violent love outran my slower-moving reason. Here lay Duncan, his pale skin streaked with blood, and his deep wounds looked like rips in life's wall where death had invaded. There were the murderers, stained with the bloody

Steeped in the colours of their trade, their daggers
Unmannerly breeched with gore: who could refrain,
That had a heart to love, and in that heart
Courage to make's love known?

130 **Lady Macbeth**   [*Seeming to faint*] Help me hence, ho!

Macduff   Look to the lady.

Malcolm   [*Aside*]   Why do we hold our tongues,
That most may claim this argument for ours?

Donalbain   What should be spoken here, where our fate,
135 Hid in an auger-hole, may rush and seize us?
Let's away.
Our tears are not yet brewed.

Malcolm   Nor our strong sorrow
Upon the foot of motion.

140 **Banquo**   Look to the lady.

And when we have our naked frailties hid,
That suffer in exposure, let us meet,
And question this most bloody piece of work,
To know it further. Fears and scruples shake us:
145 In the great hand of God I stand, and thence
Against the undivulged pretence I fight
Of treasonous malice.

Macduff   And so do I.

All   So all.

150 **Macbeth**   Let's briefly put on manly readiness.
And meet i'th'hall together.

All   Well contented.

[*Exeunt all but **Malcolm** and **Donalbain***]

color of their trade, with their daggers brutally covered with blood. Who could hold back, that had love in his heart and the courage to show that love?

Lady Macbeth [*seeming to faint*] Help me out of here! Please!

Macduff Help the lady.

Malcolm [*privately to* **Donalbain**] Why do we remain silent, when this business most concerns us?

Donalbain [*privately to* **Malcolm**] What should we say here, where our fate waits in ambush and may attack us? Let's go. We haven't yet had time for weeping.

Malcolm [*privately to* **Donalbain**] Nor has our great grief had time to act.

Banquo Help the lady.

[**Lady Macbeth** *is helped offstage*]

And when we have clothed our bodies that shiver from the cold in our nightclothes, let us meet and discuss this bloody business, so we can know more about it. Fears and doubts shake us. I put myself in God's great hand, and with God's help I will fight against the unknown purpose behind this evil treason.

Macduff And so will I.

All And so will we all.

Macbeth Let's quickly dress for action and meet in the hall.

All We are agreed.

[*All exit except* **Malcolm** *and* **Donalbain**]

Malcolm   What will you do? Let's not consort with them:
    To show an unfelt sorrow is an office
155   Which the false man does easy. I'll to England.

Donalbain   To Ireland, I: our separated fortune
    Shall keep us both the safer: where we are
    There's daggers in men's smiles: the near in blood,
    The nearer bloody.

160 **Malcolm**   This murderous shaft that's shot
    Hath not yet lighted, and our safest way
    Is to avoid the aim. Therefore to horse,
    And let us not be dainty of leave-taking,
    But shift away: there's warrant in that theft
165   Which steals itself when there's no mercy left.

[*Exeunt*]

Malcolm   What will you do? Let's not join them. It's easy for a traitor to show a sorrow he doesn't feel. I'm going to England.

Donalbain   I'll go to Ireland. We will be safer if we separate. Here, men's smiles hide daggers. The nearer they are related to us, the better reason they have to kill us.

Malcolm   This murder is not the end. To be safe, we must stay out of range. Therefore, let's get our horses and not be too fussy about good-byes, but just steal away. There's good reason for flight when there's no mercy left.

[**Malcolm** *and* **Donalbain** *exit*]

Act II

Scene IV

Before Macbeth's castle. Enter **Ross** *with an* **Old Man.**

Old Man   Threescore and ten I can remember well,
Within the volume of which time I have seen
Hours dreadful and things strange; but this sore night
Hath trifled former knowings.

5 **Ross**   Ha, good father,
Thou seest the heavens, as troubled with man's act,
Threatens his bloody stage: by th' clock 'tis day,
And yet dark night strangles the travelling lamp:
Is't night's predominance, or the day's shame,
10   That darkness does the face of earth entomb,
When living light should kiss it?

Old Man   'Tis unnatural,
Even like the deed that's done. On Tuesday last
A falcon towering in her pride of place
15   Was by a mousing owl hawked at and killed.

Ross   And Duncan's horses – a thing most strange and
     certain –
Beauteous and swift, the minions of their race,
Turned wild in nature, broke their stalls, flung out,
20   Contending 'gainst obedience, as they would make
War with mankind.

Old Man   'Tis said they eat each other.

Outside Macbeth's castle. **Ross** *and an* **Old Man** *enter.*

Old Man I can remember back seventy years, and in all that time I have seen dreadful hours and strange things. But this terrible night has made these other experiences seem like nothing.

Ross Ah, good old man, the heavens threaten the earth, troubled by the bloody deeds men perform there. By the clock, it's day, but dark night still chokes off the sun. Is it the night's strength or the day's shame that darkness still covers the face of the earth when sunlight should kiss it?

Old Man It's unnatural, even like the deed that was done. Last Tuesday, a hawk flying high in the air was attacked and killed by an owl hunting mice.

Ross And—strange but true!—Duncan's horses, beautiful and swift, the best of their kind, broke down their stalls and ran wild. They refused to obey, as if they were at war with mankind. `

Old Man People say they ate each other.

Ross   They did so, to th'amazement of mine eyes,
That looked upon't.

[*Enter* **Macduff**]

25   Here comes the good Macduff.
How goes the world, sir, now?

Macduff   Why, see you not?

Ross   Is't known who did this more than bloody deed?

Macduff   Those that Macbeth hath slain.

30 **Ross**   Alas, the day!
What good could they pretend?

Macduff   They were suborned.
Malcolm and Donalbain, the king's two sons,
Are stol'n away and fled, which puts upon them
35   Suspicion of the deed.

Ross   'Gainst nature still!
Thriftless ambition, that wilt ravin up
Thine own life's means! Then 'tis most like
The sovereignty will fall upon Macbeth.

40 **Macduff**   He is already named, and gone to Scone
To be invested.

Ross   Where is Duncan's body?

Macduff   Carried to Colmekill,
The sacred storehouse of his predecessors,
45   And guardian of their bones.

Ross   Will you to Scone?

Macduff   No cousin, I'll to Fife.

Ross   Well, I will thither.

Ross They did so, to my amazed eyes. I saw them!

[**Macduff** *enters*]

Here comes the good Macduff. [*To* **Macduff**] How are things going now, sir?

Macduff Why, can't you see?

Ross Is it known who did this worse-than-bloody deed?

Macduff The men Macbeth killed.

Ross A sad day. What could they hope to gain?

Macduff They were bribed. Malcolm and Donalbain, the king's two sons, have stolen away and fled, which makes them look suspicious.

Ross Another unnatural event! Wasteful ambition eats up what gives it life! Then it's most likely Macbeth will become king.

Macduff He has already been chosen king and gone to Scone to be crowned.

Ross Where is Duncan's body?

Macduff It was taken to Colmekill, the holy tomb where the royal family are buried.

Ross Will you go to Scone?

Macduff No, cousin, I'm going home to Fife.

Ross Well, I'm going to Scone.

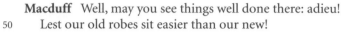

Macduff Well, may you see things well done there: adieu!
50   Lest our old robes sit easier than our new!

Ross Farewell, father.

Old Man God's benison go with you, and with those
    That would make good of bad and friends of foes!

[*Exeunt*]

Macduff   I hope you see good things happen there. But farewell, in case the future turns out to be worse than the past.

Ross   Farewell, old man.

Old Man   God's blessing go with you, and with those that would make good out of bad, and friends out of enemies.

[*They exit*]

Comprehension Check What You Know

1. How does Macbeth attempt to gain Banquo's support? How does Banquo respond?

2. What does Macbeth see as he prepares to kill the King? What conclusion does he come to about what he sees?

3. In Scene 2, why is Macbeth so troubled by his inability to say, "Amen," when he overhears one of Duncan's sons say, "God bless us!"? How does Lady Macbeth react to Macbeth's uneasiness?

4. Why is Lady Macbeth upset that Macbeth has brought the knives back with him? How does she fix the problem? Compare the way that Macbeth and Lady Macbeth react to the murder.

5. In Scene 3, who does the drunken Porter imagine he is? His comments add some humor to a very dark scene, but they also may be indicators of the evil that is overtaking the play. Read his speeches to find these indications.

6. How do Macduff's and Banquo's reactions differ when the King's murder is discovered?

7. How does Macbeth explain why he killed Duncan's servants?

8. Why do Malcolm and Donalbain decide to flee? How do the other thanes respond to their flight?

9. In Scene 4, what do the Old Man and Ross think about the strange events that have been taking place in nature?

10. How does Macduff explain the seemingly senseless murder of Duncan by his servants?

©Robbie Jack/CORBIS

Activities & Role-Playing   Classes or Informal Groups

Knock, Knock! Go through Act 2 carefully, and note places where the play requires some sort of sound effects, even if it isn't mentioned in the text. Is there high wind? How does the knock on the door sound? Do you hear Macbeth's footsteps before he joins Lady Macbeth? How much clatter is there when Macduff and Lennox enter the castle? Decide how to make the sounds.

Lady Macbeth on Trial Was Lady Macbeth as guilty of the King's death as her husband? Take the parts of Lady Macbeth, judge, prosecutor, defense lawyer, and witnesses, and role-play her trial for the crime.

Discussion   Classes or Informal Groups

1. When Lady Macbeth returns from drugging Duncan's servants, she says she would have killed the King if he hadn't looked like her father while he slept. Discuss whether Lady Macbeth could have committed this murder.

2. Take the words of the drunken Porter in Scene 3 seriously. The porter says that if he were guarding the gates of hell, he'd take his time opening up. Those words would remind Shakespeare's audience of old *morality plays,* where a porter *does* guard the gates of hell. A reference like this is called an *allusion.* It reminds people of ideas that the author doesn't want to spell out.

    Here audience members would know that Macbeth's castle has become a terrible place. What events have made Macbeth's house a place of great evil? Do not limit yourself to the murder itself. What other perspectives or events contribute to the idea of great evil?

3. In Act 2 the actors refer to sounds and sights—omens. Some have deep roots in folklore. For example, a hooting owl or chirping crickets were supposed to be omens of death. Discuss the omens in Act 2 and how they affect the way you respond to simple statements by honest people.

Suggestions for Writing   Improve Your Skills

1. *Macbeth* is a kind of horror story, complete with dark and stormy nights, witches, ghosts, bloody deeds, and the like. Pick a scene and rewrite it as a parody of a horror story.

2. In Scene 1, when Macbeth talks about killing Duncan, he thinks of "withered Murder" as a person creeping up on his victims. Describing a thing or an action as if it were a person is called *personification.* Write a short personification of some feeling, such as Anger, Guilt, Joy, or Innocence. How would this "character" behave? What would it look like? How old would it be? Would it be male or female?

All the World's a Stage Introduction

How bad is Macbeth? What's your opinion of him as a villain at this point? So far, Macbeth has shown some sympathetic qualities. Although he has committed a terrible murder, he has also been brave in battle, affectionate with his wife, and seemed to hesitate and feel regret about his acts. However, the Witches have tempted his terrible weakness—his ambition. Good and evil seem to struggle in this haunted man. In Act 3, that struggle will continue—and things don't look promising for Macbeth's "good" side.

Now that Macbeth is king, Scotland's well-being lies in his hands. In Act 3, we'll begin to hear reports from the Scottish nobles about him as a ruler.

What's in a Name? Characters

The Witches' messages pleased Macbeth. But Banquo also received good news. Macbeth may be king *now,* but the Witches foretold that Banquo's children would be kings in the future. Banquo already has a son, Fleance. And Macbeth is beginning to worry about these two.

After Duncan's death, the Scottish nobles felt uneasy in Macbeth's home, even though the "culprits" were caught and killed. Banquo seemed nervous, Malcolm and Donalbain fled, and Macduff was mistrustful and gloomy. Macbeth has attained the highest position in Scotland, but he is more and more isolated from his country's nobles—even from his wife. In Scene 1, we'll find Macbeth associating with the lowest of the low—two Murderers.

There is another frightening figure in Act 3: Macbeth is visited by a ghost. Although it has no lines and is not even listed as a character, its presence looms large as the Macbeths wine and dine their country's top citizens. As you read Scene 4, pay attention to who sees the Ghost and who does not. Decide whether you think the Ghost is "real" or whether it might be the product of a wrongdoer's guilty conscience.

COME WHAT MAY Things to Watch For

Macbeth's world is full of suspicion and freakish events. People have heard voices wailing in the wind, winds that blew hard enough to knock down chimneys. There have been bad omens, too—bird cries in the night and horses going wild. Shakespeare's audiences believed that the universe was highly ordered. Respect for rank or hierarchy was key in the scheme of things. Upsetting this order could have violent consequences in the natural world and in the social or political sphere.

Shakespeare's plots often show characters acting in ways that violate rank (such as the murder of a king). This also upsets things in the earth and in the sky. In Act 3, notice how Macbeth's "unnatural" crimes are mirrored by images of fierce disorder in the natural world. Sometimes nature seems to be a *source* of evil. Images of cats, toads, rats, owls, sharks, bats, beetles, and crows reinforce an atmosphere of danger, darkness, and death.

All Our Yesterdays   Historical and Social Context

Macbeth's character allows Shakespeare to explore one of his frequent themes: the rights and responsibilities of kingship. But how does someone become king in the first place? How does a society ensure that power is passed calmly and lawfully from one ruler to the next?

When *Macbeth* was written in about 1606, England had recently passed through a potentially dangerous time. In 1603, Queen Elizabeth I died. She was childless and had not openly named her successor. When her relative King James VI of Scotland peacefully assumed the throne to become James I of England, many English people must have felt relief. *Macbeth* shows what can happen when succession is not orderly. As Act 3 begins, Macbeth is already looking over his shoulder at other contenders for the Scottish crown.

The Play's the Thing   Staging

Shakespeare doesn't include a scene of Macbeth's coronation. Instead, when Macbeth, Lady Macbeth, and their court enter early in Act 3, a *sennet* is played. This is a musical piece played by trumpets or cornets to signal a formal procession. Here it shows that Macbeth has achieved his ambition of becoming king.

Tradition has even followed the play itself. It has an ominous reputation in the theater. Bad luck is said to have surrounded *Macbeth* from its very first performance—that night the boy playing Lady Macbeth supposedly died backstage. And that was just the first piece of bad luck associated with the play. Even today, people in the theater never mention *Macbeth* by name—they call it "the Scottish play"!

My Words Fly Up   Language

Who's a real man? In Act 3's opening scene, Macbeth compares the types of men to various kinds of dogs. His brief list of dog breeds shows how to rank and classify nature. Although the word *man* meant "male adult," it could also refer to a male *servant*. So, calling someone a *man* could refer to his masculine virtues or signal that he held a low social status.

At this point in Shakespeare's play, would you say that Macbeth is the Murderers' master, or is he their equal? Is this *man* in any way still noble or heroic?

Act III

Scene I

The palace at Forres. **Banquo** *enters.*

Banquo   Thou hast it now, King, Cawdor, Glamis, all,
As the weird women promised, and I fear
Thou play'dst most foully for't: yet it was said
It should not stand in thy posterity,
5   But that myself should be the root and father
Of many kings. If there come truth from them –
As upon thee, Macbeth, their speeches shine –
Why, by the verities on thee made good,
May they not be my oracles as well,
10   And set me up in hope? But hush, no more.

[*Enter* **Macbeth,** *as King,* **Lady Macbeth,** *as Queen,*
Lennox, Ross, Lords, Ladies *and* **Attendants**]

Macbeth   Here's our chief guest.

Lady Macbeth   If he had been forgotten,
It had been as a gap in our great feast,
And all-thing unbecoming.

15   **Macbeth**   To-night we hold a solemn supper, sir,
And I'll request your presence.

Banquo   Let your highness
Command upon me, to the which my duties
Are with a most indissoluble tie
20   For ever knit.

Macbeth's palace at Forres. **Banquo** *enters.*

Banquo You have it all now—King, Cawdor, Glamis—just as the Weird Women promised, and I am afraid you did great evil to win it. But they also said the kingship would not remain in your family, and that I should be the father of many kings. If the witches spoke the truth—as they obviously did to you, Macbeth—why, judging by the truth of their predictions about you, may I not hope that what they said about me will come true as well? But hush, no more.

[*A sennet plays.* **Macbeth,** *who is now king, enters with* **Lady Macbeth,** *now queen. They are accompanied by* **Lennox, Ross, Lords, Ladies,** *and* **Attendants**]

Macbeth Here's our most important guest.

Lady Macbeth [*to* **Macbeth**] If he had been forgotten, his absence from our great feast would have been very unbecoming.

Macbeth Tonight we're holding a formal dinner, sir. I would like you to attend.

Banquo My duty must always obey whatever Your Highness commands.

Macbeth Ride you this afternoon?

Banquo   Ay, my good lord.

Macbeth We should have else desired your good advice
Which still hath been both grave and prosperous
25   In this day's council; but we'll take to-morrow.
Is't far you ride?

Banquo As far, my lord, as will fill up the time
'Twixt this and supper. Go not my horse the better,
I must become a borrower of the night
30   For a dark hour or twain.

Macbeth   Fail not our feast.

Banquo My lord, I will not.

Macbeth We hear our bloody cousins are bestowed
In England and in Ireland, not confessing
35   Their cruel parricide, filling their hearers
With strange invention: but of that to-morrow,
When therewithal we shall have cause of state
Craving us jointly. Hie you to horse: adieu,
Till you return at night. Goes Fleance with you?

40 **Banquo** Ay, my good lord: our time does call upon's.

Macbeth I wish your horses swift and sure of foot:
And so I do commend you to their backs.
Farewell.

[*Exit* **Banquo**]

Let every man be master of his time
45   Till seven at night; to make society
The sweeter welcome, we will keep ourself
Till supper-time alone: while then, God be with you!

[*All depart but* **Macbeth** *and a* **Servant**]

Macbeth   Are you planning to go out riding this afternoon?

Banquo   Yes, my good lord.

Macbeth   [*using the royal "we"*] If this weren't so, we would have liked to have had your advice in today's council meeting. It is always sound and useful. But we'll hear it tomorrow. How far are you riding?

Banquo   As far as I can in the time between now and supper, my lord. Unless my horse is faster than I expect, I'll be traveling in the dark for an hour or two.

Macbeth   Don't fail to come to our feast.

Banquo   My lord, I won't fail.

Macbeth   We hear that our murderous cousins are living in England and Ireland. They have not confessed to killing their father and are telling people wild lies. But we can talk of that tomorrow when matters of state bring us together. Hurry off to your horse. Farewell, until you return tonight. Is Fleance going with you?

Banquo   Yes, my good lord. It's time we were going.

Macbeth   May your horses carry you swiftly and safely. And so I entrust you to them. Farewell.

[**Banquo** *exits*]

[*To the rest*] Everyone may do as he likes until seven tonight. To enjoy your company even more, we'll remain alone until supper time. Until then, God be with you!

[*All exit, except* **Macbeth** *and a* **Servant**]

Sirrah, a word with you: attend those men
Our pleasure?

50 **Servant** They are, my lord, without the palace gate.

Macbeth Bring them before us.

[*The* **Servant** *goes*]

To be thus is nothing,
But to be safely thus: our fears in Banquo
Stick deep, and in his royalty of nature
55 Reigns that which would be feared. 'Tis much he dares,
And, to that dauntless temper of his mind,
He hath a wisdom that doth guide his valor
To act in safety. There is none but he
Whose being I do fear: and under him
60 My Genius is rebuked, as it is said
Mark Antony's was by Caesar. He chid the Sisters,
When first they put the name of king upon me,
And bade them speak to him; then prophet-like
They hailed him father to a line of kings:
65 Upon my head they placed a fruitless crown,
And put a barren sceptre in my gripe,
Thence to be wrenched with an unlineal hand,
No son of mine succeeding. If't be so,
For Banquo's issue have I filed my mind,
70 For them the gracious Duncan have I murdered,
Put rancours in the vessel of my peace
Only for them, and mine eternal jewel
Given to the common enemy of man,
To make them kings, the seed of Banquo kings!
75 Rather than so, come Fate into the list,
And champion me to th'utterance. Who's there?

[*The* **Servant** *enters with two* **Murderers**]

114

Come here, you. Are those men waiting?

Servant   They are, my lord. Outside the palace gate.

Macbeth   Bring them here.

[*The* **Servant** *exits*]

To be king is nothing, unless I am *safely* king. I fear Banquo deeply. There's a kingly quality in his nature that should be feared. He is very bold, and, in addition to that fearless spirit, he has a wisdom that guides his courage to act with safety. He is the only one whom I fear. When he's around, I lose my self-confidence. It's said Mark Antony responded the same way to Octavius Caesar. Banquo spoke boldly to the Weird Sisters when they first called me King, demanding that they speak to him. Then, like prophets, they greeted him as the father of a line of kings. They placed on *my* head a fruitless crown and put a barren scepter in my grasp. These things will be seized by a hand unrelated to me; no son of mine will succeed me. If this be so, then it's for Banquo's children I defiled my spirit. For them I murdered the gracious Duncan. I have poisoned my peace of mind only for them. I have given my immortal soul, that eternal jewel, to the devil to make them kings—the children of Banquo, kings! Rather than that, come Fate, into the arena, and fight me to the death! Who's there?

[*The* **Servant** *enters with two* **Murderers**]

Now go to the door, and stay there till we call.

[*Exit* **Servant**]

Was it not yesterday we spoke together?

1st Murderer   It was, so please your highness.

80 **Macbeth**   Well then, now
Have you considered of my speeches? Know
That it was he in the times past which held you
So under fortune, which you thought had been
Our innocent self: this I made good to you
85 In our last conference; passed in probation with you,
How you were borne in hand, how crossed, the instruments,
Who wrought with them, and all things else that might
To half a soul and to a notion crazed
Say 'Thus did Banquo'.

90 **1st Murderer**   You made it known to us.

Macbeth   I did so; and went further, which is now
Our point of second meeting. Do you find
Your patience so predominant in your nature,
That you can let this go? Are you so gospelled,
95 To pray for this good man, and for his issue,
Whose heavy hand hath bowed you to the grave
And beggared yours for ever?

1st Murderer   We are men, my liege.

Macbeth   Ay, in the catalogue ye go for men,
100 As hounds and greyhounds, mongrels, spaniels, curs,
Shoughs, water-rugs, and demi-wolves, are clept
All by the name of dogs: the valued file
Distinguishes the swift, the slow, the subtle,
The housekeeper, the hunter, every one
105 According to the gift which bounteous nature
Hath in him closed, whereby he does receive

[*To the* **Servant**] Now go to the door and stay there till we call.

[*The* **Servant** *exits*]

[*To the* **Murderers**] Wasn't it yesterday that we spoke together?

1st Murderer It was, Your Highness.

Macbeth Well, then, have you thought over what I told you? Now you know that it was Banquo who in the past kept you down, for which you unfairly blamed me. I made this clear to you when we talked last. I proved to you in detail how you were deceived and defeated—how it was done, who did it, and everything else. All of this tells you, "Banquo did it," as even a halfwit or a madman would agree.

1st Murderer You explained it to us.

Macbeth I did. And I went further, which is the point of our second meeting. Do you find that patience is so strong in your nature that you can let this go? Are you so pious that you will pray for this good man and for his children, whose heavy hand has burdened you till death and made your family beggars forever?

1st Murderer We are men, my lord.

Macbeth Yes, you might pass in the *list* of "men." Just as hounds, greyhounds, mongrels, spaniels, curs, lapdogs, water-dogs, and beasts that are half-wolf are all called "dogs." But a classification by quality separates each kind— the fast, the slow, the cunning, house dogs, hunting dogs— according to the gift generous nature has given it. In this way

Particular addition, from the bill
That writes them all alike: and so of men.
Now, if you have a station in the file,
110 Not i'th' worst rank of manhood, say't,
And I will put that business in your bosoms,
Whose execution takes your enemy off,
Grapples you to the heart and love of us
Who wear our health but sickly in his life,
115 Which in his death were perfect.

2nd Murderer   I am one, my liege.
Whom the vile blows and buffets of the world
Hath so incensed that I am reckless what
I do to spite the world.

120 **1st Murderer**   And I another
So weary with disasters, tugged with fortune,
That I would set my life on any chance,
To mend it, or be rid on't.

Macbeth   Both of you
125 Know Banquo was your enemy.

Both Murderers   True, my lord.

Macbeth So is he mine: and in such bloody distance,
That every minute of his being thrusts
Against my near'st of life: and though I could
130 With barefaced power sweep him from my sight,
And bid my will avouch it, yet I must not,
For certain friends that are both his and mine,
Whose loves I may not drop, but wail his fall
Who I myself struck down: and thence it is
135 That I to your assistance do make love,
Masking the business from the common eye,
For sundry weighty reasons.

2nd Murderer   We shall, my lord,
Perform what you command us.

each kind stands out in the list that calls them all "dogs." It's the same with men. Now, if you are better than the rank and file of humanity, say so, and I will give you a task. If it's carried out, you will destroy your enemy and win my lasting friendship. As long as Banquo lives I'm in bad health, but my health will be perfect when he dies.

2nd Murderer   My lord, I'm the kind of man who's so enraged by the foul blows the world's given me that I'll do anything to get back at it.

1st Murderer   And I'm another. I'm so weary with disasters, so knocked about by fortune, that I would take any risk to better my life, or end it.

Macbeth   Both of you know Banquo was your enemy.

Both Murderers   True, my lord.

Macbeth   He is my enemy as well. And he's such a close and deadly enemy that every minute he lives stabs at my heart. Though I could use my power to destroy him openly and justify it by simply saying it was my wish, I must not do so. He and I have some friends in common whose love I need. So I must mourn the death I myself will cause. That's why I ask your help to keep this business secret for various important reasons.

2nd Murderer   We shall, my lord, perform what you command us.

140 **1st Murderer**   Though our lives –

Macbeth Your spirits shine through you. Within this hour at
        most I will advise you where to plant yourselves,
        Acquaint you with the perfect spy o'th' time,
        The moment on't, for't must be done to-night,
145   And something from the palace; always thought
        That I require a clearness: and with him –
        To leave no rubs nor botches in the work –
        Fleance his son, that keeps him company,
        Whose absence is no less material to me
150   Than is his father's, must embrace the fate
        Of that dark hour. Resolve yourselves apart;
        I'll come to you anon.

    Both Murderers   We are resolved, my lord.

    Macbeth I'll call upon you straight; abide within.

[*Exeunt* **Murderers**]

155   It is concluded: Banquo, thy soul's flight,
        If it find heaven, must find it out to-night.

[*Exit*]

1st Murderer   Even if our lives—

Macbeth   [*interrupting*] Your spirit shines through. Within the
   hour, I'll instruct you where to position yourselves and tell
   you the right time to do it—for it must be done tonight and
   at some distance from the palace. Remember that I must be
   kept clear of suspicion. And to do a complete job with no
   mess left behind, Banquo's son Fleance must share his
   father's fate in that dark hour. Fleance will be with Banquo,
   and it's just as important to get rid of him. Go and make up
   your minds. I'll come to you soon.

Both Murderers   We've made up our minds to do it, my lord.

Macbeth   I'll be with you right away. Stay inside.

[*The* **Murderers** *exit*]

That's settled. Banquo, if your soul is ever to reach heaven, it
must find it tonight.

[**Macbeth** *exits*]

Act III

Scene II

Enter **Lady Macbeth** *and a* **Servant.**

Lady Macbeth   Is Banquo gone from court?

Servant   Ay, madam, but returns again to-night.

Lady Macbeth   Say to the king, I would attend his leisure
For a few words.

5   **Servant**   Madam, I will.

                                    [*He goes*]

Lady Macbeth   Nought's had, all's spent,
   Where our desire is got without content:
   'Tis safer to be that which we destroy
   Than by destruction dwell in doubtful joy.

   [*Enter* **Macbeth**]

10   How now, my lord! why do you keep alone,
   Of sorriest fancies your companions making,
   Using those thoughts which should indeed have died
   With them they think on? Things without all remedy
   Should be without regard: what's done, is done.

15   **Macbeth**   We have scotched the snake, not killed it:
   She'll close and be herself, whilst our poor malice
   Remains in danger of her former tooth.
   But let the frame of things disjoint, both the worlds suffer,

Lady Macbeth *enters with a* **Servant**.

Lady Macbeth   Has Banquo left court?

Servant   Yes, madam, but he will return tonight.

Lady Macbeth   Tell the King I would like to speak to him.

Servant   Madam, I will.

[*The* **Servant** *exits*]

Lady Macbeth   Nothing is gained, all is lost, when we get what we wanted but still lack happiness. It's better to be a victim than to live in fear on the profits of victimizing someone else.

[**Macbeth** *enters*]

How are you, my lord? Why do you stay by yourself, with wretched thoughts as your only companions? These thoughts should have died with the people they consider. We shouldn't brood about things that can't be helped. What's done is done.

Macbeth   We have only wounded the snake, not killed it. It will heal and regain its strength, and we will once again be in danger of its bite. I would rather have the universe fall apart, and heaven and earth be destroyed, than have to eat our meals

Ere we will eat our meal in fear and sleep
20   In the affliction of these terrible dreams
That shake us nightly: better be with the dead,
Whom we, to gain our peace, have sent to peace,
Than on the torture of the mind to lie
In restless ecstasy. Duncan is in his grave;
25   After life's fitful fever he sleeps well;
Treason has done his worst: nor steel, nor poison,
Malice domestic, foreign levy, nothing,
Can touch him further.

Lady Macbeth   Come on;
30   Gentle my lord, sleek o'er your rugged looks,
Be bright and jovial among your guests to-night.

Macbeth So shall I, love, and so I pray be you:
Let your remembrance apply to Banquo;
Present him eminence, both with eye and tongue:
35   Unsafe the while, that we
Must lave our honours in these flattering streams,
And make our faces vizards to our hearts,
Disguising what they are.

Lady Macbeth   You must leave this.

40 **Macbeth** O, full of scorpions is my mind, dear wife!
Thou know'st that Banquo and his Fleance lives.

Lady Macbeth But in them nature's copy's not eterne.

Macbeth There's comfort yet; they are assailable,
Then be thou jocund: ere the bat hath flown
45   His cloistered flight, ere to black Hecate's summons
The shard-borne beetle with his drowsy hums
Hath rung night's yawning peal, there shall be done
A deed of dreadful note.

Lady Macbeth   What's to be done?

in fear and suffer the terrible dreams that attack us every night. It would be better to be with the dead—whom we, to gain our peace, have sent to their peace—than to live with a tortured mind. Duncan is in his grave. His life's troubles are over; he sleeps well. Treason has done the worst it can to him. Weapons, poison, rebellion at home, foreign invasion—none of these can touch him now.

Lady Macbeth Come on, my noble lord. Look calm; don't look so troubled. Be lively and cheerful among your guests tonight.

Macbeth I will, my love, and so should you. Remember to pay special attention to Banquo. Show him favor with your looks and words. We're still not safe, and so we must make our honor look clean by washing it in streams of flattery. We must make our faces masks for our hearts, disguising what our hearts are.

Lady Macbeth You must stop this brooding!

Macbeth Oh dear wife, my mind is full of scorpions! You know that Banquo and his Fleance live.

Lady Macbeth But they won't live forever.

Macbeth That's a comforting thought. They can be handled. So, be joyful. Before the bat makes its lonely flight, before the witch-goddess calls the scaly-winged beetle to sound night's curfew with its sleepy hum, a dreadful deed shall be done.

Lady Macbeth What's to be done?

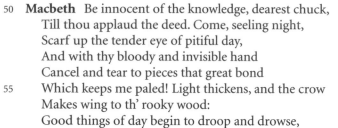

50   **Macbeth**   Be innocent of the knowledge, dearest chuck,
        Till thou applaud the deed. Come, seeling night,
        Scarf up the tender eye of pitiful day,
        And with thy bloody and invisible hand
        Cancel and tear to pieces that great bond
55   Which keeps me paled! Light thickens, and the crow
        Makes wing to th' rooky wood:
        Good things of day begin to droop and drowse,
        Whiles night's black agents to their preys do rouse.
        Thou marvell'st at my words: but hold thee still;
60   Things bad begun make strong themselves by ill:
        So, prithee, go with me.

                        [*Exeunt*]

Macbeth   Know nothing, dearest, until you applaud the deed.
Come, blinding night, blindfold the tender eye of pitying day.
With your bloody and invisible hand, cancel and tear up
Banquo's lease on life, which keeps me in fear. The light
grows dim, and the crow flies toward the dark wood. The
good things of the day begin to fall asleep, while night's
black forces wake to hunt their prey. [*To* **Lady Macbeth**] My
words amaze you, but wait. Once begun, bad things
strengthen themselves by doing more evil. So, please, come
with me.

[**Macbeth** *and* **Lady Macbeth** *exit*]

Act III

Scene III

Some way from the palace. Enter three **Murderers.**

1st Murderer But who did bid thee join with us?

3rd Murderer   Macbeth.

2nd Murderer He needs not our mistrust, since he delivers
Our offices and what we have to do,
5   To the direction just.

1st Murderer   Then stand with us.
The west yet glimmers with some streaks of day:
Now spurs the lated traveller apace
To gain the timely inn, and near approaches
10   The subject of our watch.

3rd Murderer   Hark! I hear horses.

Banquo Gives us a light there, ho!

2nd Murderer   Then 'tis he; the rest
That are within the note of expectation
15   Already are i'th' court.

1st Murderer   His horses go about.

3rd Murderer Almost a mile: but he does usually –
So all men do – from hence to th' palace gate
Make it their walk.

[*Enter* **Banquo** *and* **Fleance** *with a torch*]

A place at some distance from the palace. Three **Murderers** *enter.*

1st Murderer   But who told you to join us?

3rd Murderer   Macbeth.

2nd Murderer   [*to* **1st Murderer**] We can trust this man, because he has told us our duties and exactly what we are to do.

1st Murderer   [*to* **3rd Murderer**] Then stand with us. A few streaks of light still glimmer in the western sky. At this time of day the late traveler rides swiftly, to reach the inn in good time. The ones we're waiting for are getting near.

3rd Murderer   Listen, I hear horses.

Banquo   [*offstage*] Give us some light!

2nd Murderer   It's him. All the others that were expected are already at court.

1st Murderer   He's dismounted.

3rd Murderer   Almost a mile—but he usually does. Everyone does—they walk the mile from here to the palace gate.

[**Banquo** *and* **Fleance** *enter, carrying torches*]

20 **2nd Murderer**   A light, a light!

3rd Murderer   'Tis he.

1st Murderer Stand to't.

Banquo It will be rain tonight.

1st Murderer   Let it come down.

[*They set upon* **Banquo**]

25 **Banquo** O, treachery! Fly, good Fleance, fly, fly, fly!
    Thou mayst revenge. O slave!

[*He dies;* **Fleance** *escapes*]

3rd Murderer Who did strike out the light?

1st Murderer   Was't not the way?

3rd Murderer There's but one down; the son is fled.

30 **2nd Murderer**   We have lost
    Best half of our affair.

1st Murderer Well, let's away, and say how much is done.

[*Exeunt*]

2nd Murderer A light, a light!

3rd Murderer It's him!

1st Murderer Get ready!

Banquo It's going to rain tonight.

1st Murderer Then let it pour!

[*They attack* **Banquo**]

Banquo Oh, treachery! Run, Fleance, run! run! run! Live to revenge me! Oh, villain!

[**Banquo** *dies;* **Fleance** *escapes*]

3rd Murderer Who put out the light?

1st Murderer Wasn't that the thing to do?

3rd Murderer Only one is killed; the son got away.

2nd Murderer We've only done half the job.

1st Murderer Well, let's go and report how much we've done.

[*They exit*]

Act III

Scene IV

The hall of the palace. A banquet prepared. Enter **Macbeth, Lady Macbeth, Ross, Lennox, Lords** *and* **Attendants.**

Macbeth You know your own degrees, sit down: at first
And last the hearty welcome.

Lords Thanks to your majesty.

Macbeth Ourself will mingle with society,
5   And play the humble host:
Our hostess keeps her state, but in best time
We will require her welcome.

Lady Macbeth Pronounce it for me, sir, to all our friends,
For my heart speaks they are welcome.

[*The* **1st Murderer** *appears at the door*]

10 **Macbeth** See, they encounter thee with their hearts' thanks.
Both sides are even: here I'll sit i'th' midst:
Be large in mirth, anon we'll drink a measure
The table round. [*To* **Murderer**] There's blood upon thy face.

1st Murderer 'Tis Banquo's then.

15 **Macbeth** 'Tis better thee without than he within.
Is he dispatched?

1st Murderer My lord, his throat is cut; that I did for him.

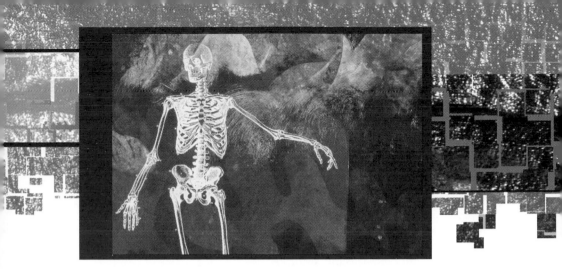

The hall of the palace. A banquet has been prepared. **Macbeth, Lady Macbeth, Ross, Lennox, Lords,** *and* **Attendants** *enter.*

Macbeth You know your ranks; sit down where you belong. To high and low, a hearty welcome!
[*They sit*]

Lords Thanks to Your Majesty.

Macbeth [*Using the royal "we"*] We will mingle with you all and play the humble host. Our hostess will stay seated. She will welcome you at the proper time.

Lady Macbeth Speak it for me, sir, to all our friends, for my heart says they are all welcome.

[*The* **1st Murderer** *enters*]

Macbeth [*to* **Lady Macbeth**] See, they respond to you with thankful hearts. There are equal numbers on both sides of the table. I'll sit here in the middle. [*He sits*] Enjoy yourselves freely. Soon we'll pass a cup around the table for a toast. [*He rises and speaks to the* **Murderer**] There's blood on your face.

1st Murderer It's Banquo's then.

Macbeth I'd rather have it on your face than in his body. Is he killed?

1st Murderer My lord, his throat is cut. I did that.

Macbeth Thou art the best o'th' cut-throats. Yet he's good
  That did the like for Fleance: if thou didst it,
20   Thou art the nonpareil.

1st Murderer   Most royal sir,
  Fleance is 'scaped.

Macbeth Then comes my fit again: I had else been perfect;
  Whole as the marble, founded as the rock,
25   As broad and general as the casing air:
  But now I am cabined, cribbed, confined, bound in
  To saucy doubts and fears. But Banquo's safe?

1st Murderer Ay, my good lord: safe in a ditch he bides,
  With twenty trenched gashes on his head;
30   The least a death to nature.

Macbeth   Thanks for that:
  There the grown serpent lies; the worm that's fled
  Hath nature that in time will venom breed,
  No teeth for th' present. Get thee gone; to-morrow
35   We'll hear ourselves again.

[*Exit* **Murderer**]

Lady Macbeth   My royal lord,
  You do not give the cheer. The feast is sold
  That is not often vouched, while 'tis a-making,
  'Tis given with welcome: to feed were best at home;
40   From thence the sauce to meat is ceremony;
  Meeting were bare without it.

[*The ghost of* **Banquo** *enters and sits in* **Macbeth**'*s place.*]

Macbeth   Sweet remembrancer!
  Now good digestion wait on appetite,
  And health on both!

45 **Lennox**   May't please your highness sit?

Macbeth You are the best of cutthroats. Yet he's just as good that did the same for Fleance. If you did it, you are without equal.

1st Murderer Most royal sir, Fleance escaped.

Macbeth Now my illness returns. Otherwise, I'd be completely sound—whole as marble, solid as rock, free as the air that surrounds us. But now I'm trapped, shut in, confined, a prisoner of persistent doubts and fears. But Banquo's taken care of?

1st Murderer Yes, my good lord. He lies safe in a ditch, with twenty deep wounds in his head, the least of them fatal.

Macbeth Thanks for that. The grown serpent lies there; the young one that got away will grow up to be poisonous. But he has no fangs yet. Leave now. We'll talk together again tomorrow.

[*The* **1st Murderer** *exits*]

Lady Macbeth My royal lord, you're not being a cheerful host. Your guests might as well be eating at an inn unless you assure them of their welcome often during the meal. If they're just eating, they would be better off at home. Away from home, good company is what makes a meal pleasant. A gathering is poor without it.

[*The ghost of* **Banquo** *enters and sits in* **Macbeth**'*s place*]

Macbeth [*to* **Lady Macbeth**] Thanks for reminding me. [*To his guests*] May good digestion follow your good appetites! And health to both!

Lennox Would Your Highness care to sit?

Macbeth Here had we now our country's honour roofed,
Were the graced person of our Banquo present;
Who may I rather challenge for unkindness
Than pity for mischance!

50 **Ross**   His absence, sir,
Lays blame upon his promise. Please't your highness
To grace us with your royal company?

Macbeth The table's full.

Lennox   Here is a place reserved, sir.

55 **Macbeth** Where?

Lennox Here, my good lord. What is't that moves your
highness?

Macbeth Which of you have done this?

Lords   What, my good lord?

60 **Macbeth** Thou canst not say I did it: never shake
Thy gory locks at me.

Ross Gentlemen, rise, his highness is not well.

Lady Macbeth Sit, worthy friends: my lord is often thus,
And hath been from his youth: pray you, keep seat,
65 The fit is momentary; upon a thought
He will again be well: if much you note him,
You shall offend him and extend his passion:
Feed, and regard him not. Are you a man?

Macbeth Ay, and a bold one, that dare look on that
70 Which might appal the devil.

Lady Macbeth   O proper stuff!
This is the very painting of your fear:
This is the air-drawn dagger which, you said,
Led you to Duncan. O, these flaws and starts
75 Impostors to true fear would well become

Macbeth We would now have all our country's nobility under one roof, if our Banquo's gracious person were present. I would rather fault him for bad manners than pity him for some misfortune.

Ross His absence, sir, is rude, because he promised. Would Your Highness please honor us with your royal company?

Macbeth The table's full.

Lennox Here is your place reserved, sir.

Macbeth Where?

Lennox Here, my good lord. What is it that upsets Your Highness?

Macbeth [*to his guests*] Which of you has done this?

Lords What, my good lord?

Macbeth [*to the* **Ghost**] You cannot say I did it. Don't shake your blood-soaked hair at me!

Ross Gentlemen, rise. His Highness is not well.

Lady Macbeth Sit, worthy friends. My lord is often this way and has been since his youth. Please, keep your seats. The attack will be over soon. In a moment he will be well again. If you pay too close attention to him, you'll offend him and prolong his attack. Eat; pay no attention to him. [*To* **Macbeth**] Are you a man?

Macbeth Yes, and a bold one, that would dare to look at that which might frighten the devil.

Lady Macbeth Oh, nonsense! This is a vision caused by your fear. This is the dagger drawn in air that you said led you to Duncan. Oh, these outbursts, these false fears, which would

A woman's story at a winter's fire,
Authorized by her grandam. Shame itself!
Why do you make such faces? When all's done,
You look but on a stool.

80 **Macbeth** Prithee, see there! behold! look! lo! how say you?
Why, what care I? If thou canst nod, speak too.
If charnel-houses and our graves must send
Those that we bury back, our monuments
Shall be the maws of kites.

[*The* **Ghost** *vanishes*]

85 **Lady Macbeth**   What! quite unmanned in folly?

Macbeth If I stand here, I saw him.

Lady Macbeth   Fie, for shame!

Macbeth Blood hath been shed ere now, i'th' olden time,
Ere humane statute purged the gentle weal;
90 Ay, and since too, murders have been performed
Too terrible for the ear: the time has been,
That, when the brains were out, the man would die,
And there an end: but now they rise again,
With twenty mortal murders on their crowns,
95 And push us from our stools. This is more strange
Than such a murder is.

Lady Macbeth   My worthy lord,
Your noble friends do lack you.

Macbeth   I do forget.
100 Do not muse at me, my most worthy friends;
I have a strange infirmity, which is nothing
To those that know me. Come, love and health to all;
Then I'll sit down. Give me some wine, fill full.

[*The* **Ghost** *returns*]

be appropriate responses to an old wives' tale at a fireside in winter! Shame on you! Why do you make such faces? After all this fuss, you're only looking at a chair.

Macbeth Look, see there! Behold, look! See, what do you say? [*To the* **Ghost**] Why, what do I care? If you can nod, speak too. If tombs and our graves will send back those we bury, we may as well leave the dead for vultures, with the birds' stomachs for their tombs.

[*The* **Ghost** *exits*]

Lady Macbeth So, is your foolishness taking away your manhood?

Macbeth As sure as I'm standing here, I saw him.

Lady Macbeth Oh, for shame!

Macbeth Blood has been shed before now, in olden days, before good laws rid the country of violence. Yes, and since then, too, murders have been done that were too terrible to be told. There was a time when, if a man's brains were beaten out, he would die, and that would be the end of him. But now the dead rise again, with twenty deadly wounds on their heads, and take our chairs from us. This is stranger than murder.

Lady Macbeth My worthy lord, your noble friends miss you.

Macbeth [*to* **Lady Macbeth**] I am forgetting. [*To the guests*] Do not wonder at me, my most worthy friends! I have a strange weakness, which is nothing to those who know me. Come, love and health to all! I'll sit down now. Give me some wine. Fill it full.

[*The* **Ghost** *enters*]

I drink to th' general joy o'th' whole table,
105   And to our dear friend Banquo, whom we miss;
Would he were here! to all, and him we thirst,
And all to all!

Lords   Our duties, and the pledge.

Macbeth   Avaunt! and quit my sight! let the earth hide thee!
110   Thy bones are marrowless, thy blood is cold;
Thou hast no speculation in those eyes
Which thou dost glare with!

Lady Macbeth   Think of this, good peers,
But as a thing of custom: 'tis no other;
115   Only it spoils the pleasure of the time.

Macbeth   What man dare, I dare:
Approach thou like the rugged Russian bear,
The armed rhinoceros, or th' Hyrcan tiger,
Take any shape but that, and my firm nerves
120   Shall never tremble: or be alive again,
And dare me to the desert with thy sword;
If trembling I inhabit then, protest me
The baby of a girl. Hence, horrible shadow!
Unreal mock'ry, hence!

[*The* **Ghost** *goes*]

125   Why, so; being gone,
I am a man again. Pray you, sit still.

Lady Macbeth   You have displaced the mirth, broke the good
     meeting,
With most admired disorder.

130   **Macbeth**   Can such things be,
And overcome us like a summer's cloud,
Without our special wonder? You make me strange
Even to the disposition that I owe,

I drink to the general joy of the whole table and to our dear friend Banquo, who is absent. If only he were here! We drink to all, and to him. Health to all!

Lords   Our duty to you and health to all.

Macbeth   [*seeing the* **Ghost**]   Begone, and leave my sight! Let the earth hide you! Your bones have no marrow, your blood is cold. You have no sight in those glaring eyes!

Lady Macbeth   [*to the guests*]   Good lords, think of this only as a chronic illness. It's nothing else. Only it's spoiling the pleasure of the evening.

Macbeth   [*to the* **Ghost**]   What any man dares, I would dare. Come at me like a rugged Russian bear, an armor-plated rhinoceros, or a fierce tiger. Take any shape but your own, and my firm nerves will never tremble. Or come to life again and challenge me to fight you in the desert. If I tremble then, call me a baby girl. Leave here, horrible shadow! Unreal mockery, away with you! [*The* **Ghost** *exits*]   Why, so. Now that it's gone, I am a man again. [*To the guests*]   Please, stay seated.

Lady Macbeth   You have ended the enjoyment, spoiled the feast with a most amazing lack of self-control.

Macbeth   Can such things happen, passing over us like a summer cloud, and not make us wonder? You make me feel

When now I think you can behold such sights,
135 And keep the natural ruby of your cheeks,
When mine is blanched with fear.

Ross   What sights, my lord?

Lady Macbeth I pray you, speak not; he grows worse and
    worse;
140 Question enrages him: at once, good night.
Stand not upon the order of your going,
But go at once.

Lennox   Good night, and better health
Attend his majesty!

145 **Lady Macbeth**   A kind good night to all!

[They leave]

Macbeth It will have blood; they say, blood will have blood:
Stones have been known to move and trees to speak;
Augures and understood relations have
By magot-pies and choughs and rooks brought forth
150 The secret'st man of blood. What is the night?

Lady Macbeth Almost at odds with morning, which is
which.

Macbeth How say'st thou, that Macduff denies his person
At our great bidding?

155 **Lady Macbeth**   Did you send to him, sir?

Macbeth I hear it by the way; but I will send:
There's not a one of them but in his house
I keep a servant fee'd. I will to-morrow,
And betimes I will, to the Weird Sisters:
160 More shall they speak; for now I am bent to know,
By the worst means, the worst. For mine own good
All causes shall give way: I am in blood

that I do not know myself. You can see such sights and keep
the natural color in your cheeks, while mine are white with fear.

Ross What sights, my lord?

Lady Macbeth Please, don't speak to him. He gets worse and
worse. Talk upsets him more. Good night to you all. Don't
take time to leave in order of rank, but depart at once.

Lennox Good night, and may His Majesty enjoy better health!

Lady Macbeth A kind good night to all of you!

[*The* **Lords** *and* **Attendants** *exit*]

Macbeth It will have blood, they say; blood will have blood.
Stones have been known to move, and trees to speak.
Magpies, jackdaws, and rooks have prophesied and made
known the most secret murderer. What time of night is it?

Lady Macbeth Sometime between night and morning. It's hard
to tell.

Macbeth What's your opinion of Macduff's refusal to come?

Lady Macbeth Have you sent for him, sir?

Macbeth I heard of his refusal indirectly; but I will send for
him. I have a servant paid to spy in every one of their homes.
Tomorrow—and early tomorrow—I will go to see the Weird
Sisters. They shall tell me more, for now I am determined to
know the worst, by the worst means. Everything must yield
to what's best for me. I stand so deep in blood that to go

Stepped in so far that, should I wade no more,
Returning were as tedious as go o'er:
165   Strange things I have in head that will to hand,
Which must be acted ere they may be scanned.

Lady Macbeth   You lack the season of all natures, sleep.

Macbeth   Come, we'll to sleep. My strange and self-abuse
Is the initiate fear that wants hard use:
170   We are yet but young in deed.

[Exeunt]

back now would be as weary as to keep on. I have strange things in my mind that must be done. They must be put into action before I have time to think about them.

Lady Macbeth You need sleep, which preserves all natures.

Macbeth Come, we'll go to sleep. My strange self-delusion tonight is the fear that comes to a beginner who needs experience. We are just getting started.

[**Macbeth** *and* **Lady Macbeth** *exit*]

Act III

Scene V

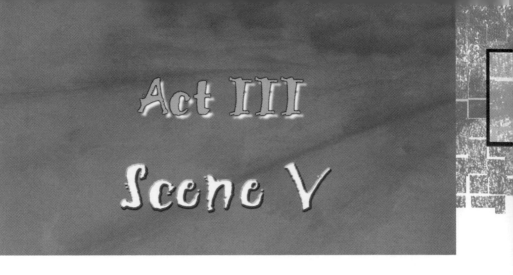

A heath. Thunder. Enter the three **Witches,** *meeting* **Hecate.**

1st Witch   Why, how now, Hecate, you look angerly.

Hecate   Have I not reason, beldams as you are,
Saucy and overbold? How did you dare
To trade and traffic with Macbeth
5   In riddles and affairs of death;
And I, the mistress of your charms,
The close contriver of all harms,
Was never called to bear my part,
Or show the glory of our art?
10   And, which is worse, all you have done
Hath been but for a wayward son,
Spiteful and wrathful, who (as others do)
Loves for his own ends, not for you.
But make amends now: get you gone,
15   And at the pit of Acheron
Meet me i'th' morning: thither he
Will come to know his destiny.
Your vessels and your spells provide,
Your charms and everything beside.
20   I am for th'air; this night I'll spend
Unto a dismal and a fatal end.
Great business must be wrought ere noon:
Upon the corner of the moon
There hangs a vap'rous drop profound:

An open field. Thunder. The three **Witches** *enter and meet* **Hecate,** *goddess of witchcraft.*

1st Witch Well now, Hecate. You look angry.

Hecate Have I not reason, you hags? How could you be so brazen and bold as to deal with Macbeth in prophecies and deadly spells? And I, the source of your power, the secret creator of all evil, was never called upon to join in and show the glory of our magic art. And what is worse, you have done all this for a willful man, who is angry and spiteful, and who, like others, seeks his own good, not yours. But make amends now. Begone, and meet me in the morning at the pit of Hell. He will come there to learn his fate. Your magic cauldrons and your spells will provide everything you need. I will fly off now. This night I'll spend causing disaster and death. Great things must be done before noon. A drop of vapor is hanging on the corner of the moon. I'll catch it before it reaches the

25   I'll catch it ere it come to ground:
     And that distilled by magic sleights
     Shall raise such artificial sprites
     As by the strength of their illusion
     Shall draw him on to his confusion.
30   He shall spurn fate, scorn death, and bear
     His hopes 'bove wisdom, grace, and fear:
     And you all know security
     Is mortals' chiefest enemy.

[*Music and a song: 'Come away, come away,'*]

     Hark, I am called: my little spirit, see,
35   Sits in a foggy cloud, and stays for me.

[*She flies away*]

1st Witch   Come, let's make haste; she'll soon be back again.

[*They vanish*]

ground. This drop, distilled with magic skills, shall produce visions of spirits that, by the power of illusion, shall bring him to destruction. He shall reject fate, scorn death, and place his ambition above wisdom, virtue, or fear. And as you know, overconfidence is humanity's greatest enemy.

[*Music plays and the song "Come away, come away" is performed*]

Listen! I am called. See where my little spirit sits in a foggy cloud and waits for me.

[**Hecate** *flies away*]

1st Witch   Come, let's hurry. She'll be back again soon.

[*They disappear*]

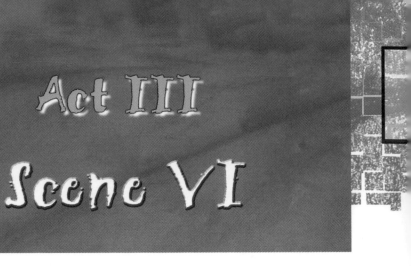

Act III

Scene VI

Forres. The Palace. Enter **Lennox** *and another* **Lord.**

Lennox   My former speeches have but hit your thoughts,
Which can interpret farther: only I say
Things have been strangely borne. The gracious Duncan
Was pitied of Macbeth: marry he was dead:
5   And the right valiant Banquo walked too late –
Whom you may say if't please you Fleance killed,
For Fleance fled: men must not walk too late.
Who cannot want the thought, how monstrous
It was for Malcolm and for Donalbain
10   To kill their gracious father? damned fact!
How it did grieve Macbeth! did he not straight,
In pious rage, the two delinquents tear,
That were the slaves of drink and thralls of sleep?
Was not that nobly done? Ay, and wisely too;
15   For 'twould have angered any heart alive
To hear the men deny't. So that, I say,
He has borne all things well: and I do think
That, had he Duncan's sons under his key –
As, an't please heaven, he shall not – they should find
20   What 'twere to kill a father; so should Fleance.
But, peace! for from broad words, and 'cause he failed
His presence at the tyrant's feast, I hear,
Macduff lives in disgrace. Sir, can you tell
Where he bestows himself?

The palace at Forres. **Lennox** *enters with another* **Lord.**

Lennox   What I've been saying agrees with your own thoughts;
you can guess the rest. I'll only add, strange things have
happened. [*Speaking with sarcasm*] The gracious Duncan
was pitied by Macbeth: Though to be sure, he was dead. And
the very brave Banquo went walking too late. You may say, if
you like, that Fleance killed him, because Fleance ran away.
Men shouldn't walk too late. Who can't help thinking how
horrible it was for Malcolm and Donalbain to kill their
gracious father? What a dreadful deed! How Macbeth
grieved over it! Didn't he immediately in a holy rage kill the
two criminals that were the slaves of drink and sleep? Wasn't
that a noble deed? Yes, and a wise one too; for it would have
angered anyone with a heart to hear the men deny the deed.
As a result, I say he has managed everything well. And I
think that if he had Duncan's sons under lock and key—which
I hope to heaven he will not—they would learn the penalty
for killing a father. So should Fleance. But enough! For I hear
that Macduff is in disgrace because he has spoken plainly
and because he failed to attend the tyrant's feast. Sir, can you
tell me where he has gone?

25 **Lord** The son of Duncan
From whom this tyrant holds the due of birth
Lives in the English court, and is received
Of the most pious Edward with such grace
That the malevolence of fortune nothing
30 Takes from his high respect. Thither Macduff
Is gone to pray the holy king, upon his aid
To wake Northumberland and warlike Siward,
That by the help of these – with Him above
To ratify the work – we may again
35 Give to our tables meat, sleep to our nights;
Free from our feasts and banquets bloody knives;
Do faithful homage and receive free honours;
All which we pine for now. And this report
Hath so exasperate the king that he
40 Prepares for some attempt of war.

Lennox Sent he to Macduff?

Lord He did: and with an absolute 'Sir, not I',
The cloudy messenger turns me his back,
And hums, as who should say, 'You'll rue the time
45 That clogs me with this answer.'

Lennox And that well might
Advise him to a caution, to hold what distance
His wisdom can provide. Some holy angel
Fly to the court of England and unfold
50 His message ere he come, that a swift blessing
May soon return to this our suffering country
Under a hand accursed!

Lord I'll send my prayers with him.

[*Exeunt*]

Lord Duncan's son, whose birthright this tyrant has stolen, lives at the English court. The most holy King Edward has welcomed him so kindly that Malcolm's fall from fortune has had no effect on how he is treated there. Macduff has gone there to plead with the holy King to aid Malcolm by rousing up the people of Northumberland and their warlike Earl, Siward. With their help—and God's will—we may again put food on our tables, sleep at night, free our feasts and banquets from bloodshed, be loyal to our lord and receive the honor of our followers—all of which we long for now. And the report of this has made Macbeth so angry that he is preparing for war.

Lennox Did he summon Macduff?

Lord He did; and when Macduff said flatly, "Sir, I won't come," the scowling messenger turned his back and grumbled, as if to say, "You'll regret the time you burdened me with this answer."

Lennox And that ought to convince Macduff to be cautious and keep a safe distance from Macbeth. May some holy angel fly to the English court and deliver Macduff's message before he gets there, so that a swift blessing may soon return to our country suffering under Macbeth's cursed hand!

Lord I'll send my prayers with him.

[**Lennox** *and the* **Lord** *exit*]

Comprehension Check What You Know

1. As Scene 1 opens, how does Banquo feel about Macbeth? Why?

2. In his soliloquy in Scene 1, lines 52–76, what is upsetting Macbeth? Why does it upset him so much?

3. How does Macbeth convince the Murderers to kill Banquo?

4. What feelings does Lady Macbeth show in Scene 2, lines 6–9?

5. Why doesn't Macbeth tell his wife about his plans for Banquo's murder? What does that tell you about their relationship?

6. What surprises the two Murderers at the beginning of Scene 3?

7. How does Macbeth react to the news of Fleance's escape? Why?

8. How many people can see Banquo's ghost during the banquet?

9. How does Lady Macbeth react to Macbeth's outburst at the banquet? What does she do to try to save the situation?

10. What noble refused to come to the feast? How do you know?

11. Scholars agree that Scene 5 is not Shakespeare. Nevertheless, what information does that scene tell you about Hecate's plans to get back at Macbeth?

12. How do some of the nobles feel about Macbeth in Scene 6?

Activities & Role-Playing Classes or Informal Groups

Bitter Banquet In Scene 3 the actors portraying Macbeth and Lady Macbeth can shine. Act out their conversation after Macbeth has first seen Banquo's ghost. (You may break the parts down into sections to allow each member of

©Robbie Jack/CORBIS

your group a chance to act.) Consider how these married partners appear to be working less well together. Who is performing poorly for the guests? Who is exhausted? What are the guests doing while the couple talks?

Witchy Work Most scholars agree that Scene 5 was written by someone other than Shakespeare. Read the scene aloud and point out any ways that you think the scene does not fit into the play. Consider the sound of the lines, the images used, and the information Hecate gives. Many modern-day productions cut this scene. Do you think this is a good or a bad idea?

Two Plus One The identity of the Third Murderer in Scene 3 has long been somewhat puzzling. Who is he? It has often been suggested that the Third Murderer is Macbeth's attendant in Scene 1 or Macbeth himself. It has also been pointed out that it's simply convenient to have a third person help carry the body and torch off stage at the end of the scene! Imagine you are the Three Murderers, getting ready to tell your employer about your success or failure. Imagine their nervous conversation. Can they trust one another? Consider who the Third Murderer might be and how the other two might question him.

Discussion   Classes or Informal Groups

1. Look at the position that Banquo is in. He has a firm conviction that Macbeth killed Duncan to get the crown. What are his options?

2. How do the guests react in the banquet scene as they watch their king scream and yell at what appears to them to be nothing? What do you think they are thinking or wondering?

3. Discuss Macbeth's character in Act 3. In what ways does he seem to be changing? What aspects of his personality are getting him into even deeper trouble?

Suggestions for Writing   Improve Your Skills

1. Banquo clearly knows too much, and he knows it. Write a letter from Banquo to his son. What information would he share? What advice would he give?

2. We have seen Macbeth getting ready to kill Duncan (Acts 1 and 2) and Banquo (Act 3). Review the scenes in all three acts in which Macbeth prepares for murder. Then write two paragraphs describing how his preparations are different for each murder and why. Pay particular attention to Macbeth's mood and helpers as he prepares to shed blood.

All the World's a Stage Introduction

Once, ruling Scotland was Macbeth's great dream. Now, that dream has turned into a nightmare. Calm, it seems, is nowhere to be found—not in Macbeth's mind or in his kingdom.

At the beginning of the play, characters told us about Macbeth's courage, even before he walked on stage. Since then, his nature has been changed by guilt and fear. Instead of stopping him, they drive him from one crime to the next in a desperate search for security. Macbeth's fear radiates outward, affecting other characters as his nightmare grows and his slide into evil continues.

What's in a Name? Characters

Who can defeat Macbeth? In Act 3, he eliminated one threat to his rule, Banquo. But Banquo's son escaped. Meanwhile, Malcolm, the legal king of Scotland, is still safe beyond Macbeth's reach.

In Act 4, we'll see more of Malcolm, legal ruler of Macbeth's kingdom. Fearing that he will be the next murder victim, he has taken refuge in England. Malcolm is "safe" there, but he knows that Macbeth still plots against him from Scotland.

When the Scottish noble Macduff reappears in the play to confer with Malcolm in Act 4, Malcolm faces a tough decision. If you were him, how might you test Macduff to see if you could trust him?

COME WHAT MAY Things to Watch For

In Act 1, Lady Macbeth spoke of nursing a child (1.7.60–61). However, now the Macbeths appear to have no children. In Shakespeare's time, it was not unusual for children to die young. (Shakespeare himself lost his son, Hamnet, at age 11.) Nevertheless, many people have wondered about what happened to the Macbeths' children.

Children are very important in *Macbeth*. In Act 4, watch for how children—or visions of them—play a role in Macbeth's fate. He has already thought much about Banquo's and Duncan's offspring, and he's unlikely to show any mercy to any man, woman, or child in his way. Children are sometimes called *issue,* because they both come from and follow their parents. Born in the present, they represent the future. And Macbeth, as we know, is anxious about his future security.

In Act 4, Macbeth will see a vision of eight kings—all the descendents (issue) of Banquo. The last is James I, who reigned over both England and Scotland at the time Shakespeare wrote *Macbeth.* By presenting James as Banquo's descendent, Shakespeare emphasized the legitimacy and longevity of James's family, the Stuarts.

All Our Yesterdays Historical and Social Context

As if Macbeth, Malcolm, and Banquo's lines weren't enough, Shakespeare also tosses in Edward the Confessor, who was England's king from 1006 to 1066. Edward is sheltering Malcolm in his court in England. In Act 4, we'll hear about his miraculous ability to cure people of a certain illness through his touch and prayers. The disease was *scrofula* (traditionally known as "the king's evil"), a condition characterized by swollen glands in the neck. In this reference, Shakespeare makes the contrast between a good king, Edward, and a bad one, Macbeth, very sharp.

The Play's the Thing Staging

"Double, double, toil and trouble"! Shakespeare cooks up a wild scene for the opening of Act 4, when Macbeth visits the Witches for advice. The scene is one of the most spectacular in all his plays. Unfortunately, we don't know a great deal about how it was originally staged. The Witches' cauldron (large pot) probably rose up through the floor on The Globe's trapdoor. The three visions, or *apparitions,* that Macbeth sees probably rose up through the cauldron.

Other plays with witches can give us some clues on staging. Ben Jonson, another Elizabethan playwright, wrote *The Masque of Queens.* This play featured witches singing and dancing. Jonson's witches danced back-to-back in circles, moving to the *left,* or sinister, side. This was considered an evil direction because it was counter to the way the sun moves across the sky. Shakespeare's Witches may have moved the same way.

My Words Fly Up Language

Shakespeare had an enormous vocabulary to choose from, so it's a good idea to pay attention when he repeats certain words. In *Macbeth,* one such word is *fear.* In fact, *fear* occurs more in *Macbeth* than in any other Shakespeare play, which fits the play's mood. Another word that appears often in *Macbeth* is *tyrant.* After Macbeth comes to power, those who oppose him almost always refer to him as a *tyrant* and to his rule as *tyranny.* (To dominate like a tyrant is to *tyrannize.*) These words show that Macbeth's act of murder did not make him into a true king.

When Macbeth sees a vision of the long line of kings in Scene 1, he notes that some hold "two-fold balls and treble scepters" (line 133). Like a crown, balls and scepters symbolize royal powers that are given to a ruler at coronation. The "two-fold balls" probably refer to King James's two coronations—one in Scotland and one in England. The "treble scepters" may point to James's claim to be ruler of Great Britain, Ireland, and France.

Act IV

Scene I

A cavern and in the middle a fiery cauldron. Thunder. Enter the three **Witches.**

1st Witch Thrice the brinded cat hath mewed.

2nd Witch Thrice and once the hedge-pig whined.

3rd Witch Harpier cries: 'Tis time, 'tis time.

1st Witch Round about the cauldron go:
5   In the poisoned entrails throw.
       Toad, that under cold stone
       Days and nights has thirty-one
       Sweltered venom sleeping got,
       Boil thou first i'th' charmed pot!

10 **All** Double, double toil and trouble;
       Fire burn and cauldron bubble.

       2nd Witch Fillet of a fenny snake,
       In the cauldron boil and bake:
       Eye of newt and toe of frog,
15   Wool of bat and tongue of dog,
       Adder's fork and blind-worm's sting,
       Lizard's leg and howlet's wing,
       For a charm of powerful trouble,
       Like a hell-broth boil and bubble.

20 **All** Double, double toil and trouble;
       Fire burn and cauldron bubble.

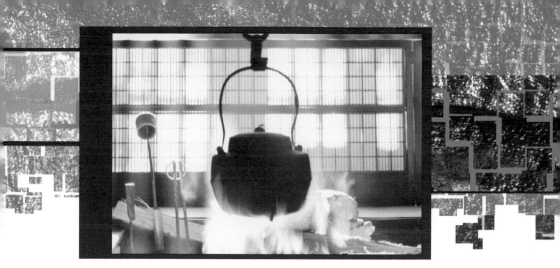

A cave. In the center, there is a boiling cauldron (large pot).
Thunder. The three **Witches** *enter.*

1st Witch   The striped cat has meowed three times.

2nd Witch   The hedgehog whined three times plus one.

3rd Witch   My demon cries, "It's time, it's time!"

1st Witch   [*chanting*] All around the pot let's go;
In it poison guts we throw.
And boil a toad that thirty-one
Days and nights, beneath cold stone,
Slept while poison sweat oozed out.
Let's boil them first in the charmed pot.

All   [*circling and chanting around the pot*]
Double, double, toil and trouble.
Fire burn and cauldron bubble.

2nd Witch   Throw a slice of swampy snake
In the pot to boil and bake;
Add eye of newt and toe of frog,
Fur of bat and tongue of dog,
Snake's forked tongue and blindworm's sting,
Lizard's leg and young owl's wing,
For a charm of powerful trouble,
Must like hell's broth boil and bubble.

All   Double, double, toil and trouble.
Fire burn and cauldron bubble.

3rd Witch Scale of dragon, tooth of wolf,
Witch's mummy, maw and gulf
Of the ravined salt-sea shark,
25   Root of hemlock digged i'th' dark,
Liver of blaspheming Jew,
Gall of goat and slips of yew
Slivered in the moon's eclipse,
Nose of Turk and Tartar's lips,
30   Finger of birth-strangled babe
Ditch-delivered by a drab,
Make the gruel thick and slab:
Add thereto a tiger's chaudron,
For th'ingredience of our cauldron.

35   **All** Double, double toil and trouble;
Fire burn and cauldron bubble.

2nd Witch Cool it with a baboon's blood,
Then the charm is firm and good.

[*Enter* **Hecate**]

Hecate O, well done! I commend your pains,
40   And every one shall shall i'th' gains:
And now about the cauldron sing,
Like elves and fairies in a ring,
Enchanting all that you put in.

[*Music and a song: Black spirits.* **Hecate** *goes*]

2nd Witch By the pricking of my thumbs,
45   Something wicked this way comes:
Open, locks,
Whoever knocks!

[*Enter* **Macbeth**]

3rd Witch   Add dragon's scale and add wolf's claw,
Bits of mummy, stomach and maw
Of a savage salt-sea shark,
Root of a hemlock dug by dark,
Liver of an evil Jew,
Gall of goat and twigs of yew
Cut off in the moon's eclipse,
Nose of Turk and Tartar's lips,
Thumb of babe that in a rut
Was birthed and strangled by a slut.
To make the soup grow thick and clot,
Add tiger's guts to what we've got
For the ingredients of our pot.

All   Double, double, toil and trouble.
Fire burn and cauldron bubble.

2nd Witch   Cool it with a baboon's blood,
Then the spell is firm and good.

[**Hecate** *enters*]

Hecate   Oh, well done! I approve your pains,
And everyone shall share the gains.
And now about the cauldron sing,
Like elves and fairies in a ring,
Enchanting all that you put in.

[*There is music and a song, "Black Spirits."* **Hecate** *exits*]

2nd Witch   By the pricking of my thumbs,
Something wicked this way comes.
Open locks, whoever knocks!

[**Macbeth** *enters*]

Macbeth How now, you secret, black, and midnight hags!
What is't you do?

50 **All**   A deed without a name.

Macbeth I conjure you, by that which you profess
Howe'er you come to know it answer me:
Though you untie the winds and let them fight
Against the churches; though the yesty waves
55 Confound and swallow navigation up;
Though bladed corn be lodged and trees blown down;
Though castles topple on their warder's heads;
Though palaces and pyramids do slope
Their heads to their foundations; though the treasure
60 Of Nature's germens tumble all together,
Even till destruction sicken; answer me
To what I ask you.

1st Witch   Speak.

2nd Witch   Demand.

65 **3rd Witch**   We'll answer.

1st Witch Say if th'hadst rather hear it from our mouths,
Or from our masters.

Macbeth   Call 'em, let me see 'em!

1st Witch Pour in sow's blood, that hath eaten
70 Her nine farrow; grease that's sweaten
From the murderer's gibbet throw
Into the flame.

All   Come, high or low;
Thyself and office deftly show.

[*Thunder.* **First Apparition:** *an armed head*]

75 **Macbeth** Tell me, thou unknown power –

Macbeth Well now, you midnight hags that deal in secrets and black magic, what are you doing?

All A deed without a name.

Macbeth I call upon you—by the black art you practice, however you come to know it—to answer me. Although you let loose the winds and let them fight against the churches, though the foamy waves sink and swallow up ships, though the ripe grain is flattened and trees are blown down, though castles fall on their guards' heads, though the tops of palaces and pyramids bend down to their foundations, though the seeds of existence all tumble and mix until even destruction grows sick of it all—answer what I ask you.

1st Witch Speak.

2nd Witch Demand.

3rd Witch We'll answer.

1st Witch Tell us whether you would rather hear it from our mouths or from our masters.

Macbeth Call them. Let me see them.

1st Witch Pour in blood of sow that ate
Of her nine piglets, add the sweated
Grease from a killer's gallows. Feed the flame!

All Come spirits high and low,
Yourselves and your works deftly show!

[*Thunder. The* **1st Apparition** *appears. It is a head in armor*]

Macbeth Tell me, you unknown power—

1st Witch   He knows thy thought:
  Hear his speech, but say thou nought.

1st Apparition Macbeth! Macbeth! Macbeth! beware
        Macduff,
80 Beware the thane of Fife. Dismiss me. Enough.

                                        [*Descends*]

Macbeth Whate'er thou art, for thy good caution thanks;
  Thou hast harped my fear aright. But one word more –

1st Witch He will not be commanded: here's another,
  More potent than the first.

  [*Thunder.* **Second Apparition:** *a bloody child*]

85 **2nd Apparition** Macbeth! Macbeth! Macbeth!

Macbeth Had I three ears, I'd hear thee.

2nd Apparition Be bloody, bold, and resolute: laugh to scorn
  The power of man; for none of woman born
  Shall harm Macbeth.

                                        [*Descends*]

90 **Macbeth** Then live, Macduff: what need I fear of thee?
  But yet I'll make assurance double sure,
  And take a bond of fate: thou shalt not live,
  That I may tell pale-hearted fear it lies,
  And sleep in spite of thunder.

  [*Thunder.* **Third Apparition:** *a child crowned, with a tree
  in his hand*]

95   What is this,
  That rises like the issue of a king,
  And wears upon his baby-brow the round
  And top of sovereignty?

1st Witch He knows your thoughts. Hear what he speaks, but say nothing.

1st Apparition Macbeth! Macbeth! Macbeth! Beware Macduff, beware the Thane of Fife. Dismiss me. Enough.

[*The* **1st Apparition** *descends*]

Macbeth Whatever you are, thanks for your good warning; you have correctly touched on my fear. But one more question—

1st Witch He will not be commanded. Here's another, more powerful than the first.

[*Thunder. The* **2nd Apparition** *appears. It is a child covered in blood*]

2nd Apparition Macbeth! Macbeth! Macbeth!

Macbeth If I had three ears, I'd hear you.

2nd Apparition Be bloody, bold, and determined; laugh to scorn the power of man, for no one born of woman shall harm Macbeth.

[*The* **2nd Apparition** *descends*]

Macbeth Then live, Macduff; why should I fear you? But I'll make my security doubly safe and get a guarantee from fate. You shall not live, Macduff, so that I may despise my fear, and sleep through thunder.

[*Thunder. The* **3rd Apparition** *appears. It is a child wearing a crown and holding a tree in his hand*]

What is this that rises looking like a king's child and wearing a crown on its infant head?

All   Listen, but speak not to't.

100 **3rd Apparition**   Be lion-mettled, proud, and take no care
Who chafes, who frets, or where conspirers are:
Macbeth shall never vanquished be until
Great Birnam wood to high Dunsinane hill
Shall come against him.

[*Descends*]

105 **Macbeth**   That will never be;
Who can impress the forest, bid the tree
Unfix his earth-bound root? Sweet bodements! good.
Rebellious dead, rise never, till the wood
Of Birnam rise, and our high-placed Macbeth
110 Shall live the lease of nature, pay his breath
To time and mortal custom. Yet my heart
Throbs to know one thing; tell me, if your art
Can tell so much: shall Banquo's issue ever
Reign in this kingdom?

115 **All**   Seek to know no more.

Macbeth   I will be satisfied: deny me this,
And an eternal curse fall on you! Let me know –

[*The cauldron descends*]

Why sinks that cauldron? and what noise is this?

1st Witch   Show!

120 **2nd Witch**   Show!

3rd Witch   Show!

All   Show his eyes, and grieve his heart;
Come like shadows, so depart.

[*A show of eight* **Kings,** *the last with a glass in his hand;*
Banquo's Ghost *following*]

All Listen, but don't speak to it.

3rd Apparition Be lion-hearted, proud, and don't worry about who is irritated or discontented or where the plotters are. Macbeth shall never be defeated until great Birnam Wood shall come against him at Dunsinane Hill.

[*The* **3rd Apparition** *descends*]

Macbeth That will never happen. Who can order a forest to march, command the tree to pull his roots from the ground? Sweet predictions! Good. Dead rebels, if you never rise till Birnam Wood rises, then royal Macbeth shall live out his natural life until time and death make him breathe his last. Yet my heart yearns to know one thing: shall Banquo's children ever reign in this kingdom?

All Seek to know no more.

Macbeth I demand to be satisfied. Deny me this, and may an eternal curse fall on you! Let me know.

[*The cauldron descends; music plays*]

Why is the cauldron sinking? And what is that music?

1st Witch Show!

2nd Witch Show!

3rd Witch Show!

All Show his eyes, and grieve his heart;
Come like shadows, then depart!

[*One by one, a procession of eight* **Kings** *appears. The last king carries a mirror in his hand.* **Banquo's Ghost** *follows them*]

Macbeth Thou art too like the spirit of Banquo: down!
125 Thy crown does sear mine eye-balls. And thy hair,
Thou other gold-bound brow, is like the first.
A third is like the former. Filthy hags!
Why do you show me this? – A fourth? Start, eyes!
What, will the line stretch out to th' crack of doom?
130 Another yet? A seventh? I'll see no more:
And yet the eighth appears, who bears a glass
Which shows me many more; and some I see
That two-fold balls and treble sceptres carry.
Horrible sight! Now I see 'tis true,
135 For the blood-boltered Banquo smiles upon me,
And points at them for his. What, is this so?

1st Witch Ay, sir, all this is so. But why
Stands Macbeth thus amazedly?
Come, sisters, cheer we up his spirits,
140 And show the best of our delights.
I'll charm the air to give a sound,
While you perform your antic round:
That this great king may kindly say
Our duties did his welcome pay.

[*Music. The* **Witches** *dance, and vanish*]

145 **Macbeth** Where are they? Gone? Let this pernicious hour
Stand aye accursed in the calendar
Come in, without there!

[*Enter* **Lennox**]

Lennox   What's your grace's will?

Macbeth Saw you the Weird Sisters?

150 **Lennox**   No, my lord.

Macbeth Came they not by you?

Macbeth [*to the first king*] You are too much like Banquo's ghost. Down! Your crown sears my eyes. [*To the second*] And your hair, also crowned with gold, is like the first. [*A third appears*] A third is like the others. [*To the* **Witches**] Filthy hags, why do you show me this? [*A fourth appears*] A fourth? My eyes will burst! [*A fifth and sixth appear*] What, will the line stretch out to eternity? [*A seventh appears*] Another yet? A seventh? [*To the* **Witches**] I'll see no more. [*An eighth appears*] And yet the eighth appears, who carries a mirror that shows me many more; and some I see carry emblems of a greater kingship. Horrible sight! Now I see it's true, for blood-spattered Banquo smiles at me and indicates these kings are his. [*The apparitions disappear*] What—is this so?

1st Witch Yes, sir, all this is so. But why does Macbeth stand so amazed? Come sisters, let's cheer up his spirits, and show the best of our delights. I'll charm the air to give music, while you prance and dance around, so this great king may kindly say that we repaid his welcome well.

[*Music. The* **Witches** *dance and then vanish*]

Macbeth Where are they? Gone? Let this evil hour stand forever cursed in the calendar! Come in, you standing outside!

[**Lennox** *enters*]

Lennox What does Your Grace wish?

Macbeth Did you see the Weird Sisters?

Lennox No, my lord.

Macbeth They didn't pass by you?

Lennox   No indeed, my lord.

Macbeth Infected be the air whereon they ride,
  And damned all those that trust them! I did hear
155 The galloping of horse. Who was't came by?

Lennox 'Tis two or three, my lord, that bring you word
  Macduff is fled to England.

Macbeth   Fled to England!

Lennox Ay, my good lord.

160 **Macbeth** Time, thou anticipat'st my dread exploits:
  The flighty purpose never is o'ertook
  Unless the deed go with it. From this moment
  The very firstlings of my heart shall be
  The firstlings of my hand. And even now
165 To crown my thoughts with acts, be it thought and done:
  The castle of Macduff I will surprise,
  Seize upon Fife, give to th'edge o'th'sword
  His wife, his babes, and all unfortunate souls
  That trace him in his line. No boasting like a fool;
170 This deed I'll do before this purpose cool.
  But no more sights! Where are these gentlemen?
  Come, bring me where they are.

                               [*Exeunt*]

Lennox   No indeed, my lord.

Macbeth   May the air they ride upon be infected and all who trust them be damned! I heard the galloping of horses. Who came by?

Lennox   It's two or three men, my lord, bringing you word that Macduff has fled to England.

Macbeth   Fled to England!

Lennox   Yes, my good lord.

Macbeth   [*to himself*] Time, you hinder my dreadful deeds. Our purposes always escape us unless we act on them at once. From this moment, my first impulses will be accompanied by quick deeds. And to complete my thoughts with acts right away, let this be thought and done: I will attack Macduff's castle without warning, seize Fife, and put to the sword his wife, his children, and his whole unfortunate family. I won't boast like a fool; I'll do this before my temper cools. But no more visions! [*To* **Lennox**] Where are these gentlemen? Come, take me to them.

[**Macbeth** *and* **Lennox** *exit*]

Act IV

Scene II

Fife. Macduff's castle. Enter **Lady Macduff,** *her* **Son,** *and* **Ross.**

Lady Macduff   What had he done, to make him fly the land?

Ross   You must have patience, madam.

Lady Macduff   He had none:
His flight was madness: when our actions do not,
5   Our fears do make us traitors.

Ross   You know not
Whether it was his wisdom or his fear.

Lady Macduff   Wisdom! to leave his wife, to leave his babes,
His mansion and his titles, in a place
10   From whence himself does fly? He loves us not;
He wants the natural touch: for the poor wren,
The most diminutive of birds, will fight,
Her young ones in her nest, against the owl.
All is the fear and nothing is the love;
15   As little is the wisdom, where the flight
So runs against all reason.

Ross   My dearest coz,
I pray you school yourself. But, for your husband,
He is noble, wise, judicious, and best knows
20   The fits o'th'season. I dare not speak much further,
But cruel are the times, when we are traitors
And do not know ourselves; when we hold rumour

Fife. Macduff's Castle. **Lady Macduff,** *her* **Son,** *and* **Ross**
enter.

Lady Macduff   What had he done to make him flee the country?

Ross   You must have patience, madam.

Lady Macduff   He had none. His flight was madness. Our fears
make us traitors, even when our actions do not.

Ross   You don't know whether it was his wisdom or his fear.

Lady Macduff   Wisdom? To leave his wife, to leave his children,
his estate, and his possessions in a place from which he
himself has fled? He doesn't love us. He lacks natural
feelings. Even the poor wren, the tiniest of birds, will fight
against the owl to protect the young ones in her nest. This is
all fear; there is no love. No wisdom either, when flight is so
unreasonable.

Ross   My dearest cousin, please control yourself. As for your
husband, he is noble, wise, prudent, and understands the
violence of the times. I don't dare speak much further. These
are cruel times, when we are traitors without knowing it. We
believe every rumor because of our own fears. Yet we don't

From what we fear, yet know not what we fear,
But float upon a wild and violent sea,
25   Each way and more. I take my leave of you:
Shall not be long but I'll be here again:
Things at the worst will cease, or else climb upward
To what they were before. My pretty cousin,
Blessing upon you!

30 **Lady Macduff** Fathered he is, and yet he's fatherless.

Ross I am so much a fool, should I stay longer
It would be my disgrace and your discomfort.
I take my leave at once.

                    [*Exit*]

Lady Macduff   Sirrah, your father's dead,
35   And what will you do now? How will you live?

Son As birds do, mother.

Lady Macduff   What, with worms and flies?

Son With what I get, I mean, and so do they.

Lady Macduff Poor bird! thou'ldst never fear the net nor
40   lime,
The pitfall nor the gin.

Son Why should I, mother? Poor birds they are not set for.
My father is not dead, for all your saying.

Lady Macduff Yes, he is dead: how wilt thou do for a father?

45 **Son** Nay, how will you do for a husband?

Lady Macduff Why, I can buy me twenty at any market.

Son Then you'll buy'em to sell again.

Lady Macduff Thou speak'st with all thy wit, and yet i'faith
With wit enough for thee.

50 **Son** Was my father a traitor, mother?

know what we fear, but float upon a wild and violent sea, tossed this way and that. I bid you goodbye. It won't be long before I'll be here again. These troubles will either cease or mount again. My pretty cousin, blessing upon you!

Lady Macduff [*Looking toward her son*] He has a father, but he's fatherless.

Ross I am such a fool, that if I stay longer, I will disgrace myself and make you uncomfortable by weeping. I will leave at once.

[**Ross** *exits*]

Lady Macduff Child, your father's dead, and what will you do now? How will you live?

Son As birds do, Mother.

Lady Macduff What, by eating worms and flies?

Son With what I can get, I mean, just like they do.

Lady Macduff Poor bird! You would never fear nets or snares, pitfalls or traps?

Son Why should I, Mother? They don't trap "poor" birds. My father is not dead, whatever you say.

Lady Macduff Yes, he is dead. What will you do for a father?

Son No, what will you do for a husband?

Lady Macduff Why, I can buy myself twenty at any marketplace.

Son Then you'll buy them to sell again.

Lady Macduff You speak as a child, but cleverly as well.

Son Was my father a traitor, mother?

Lady Macduff Ay, that he was.

Son What is a traitor?

Lady Macduff Why, one that swears and lies.

Son And be all traitors that do so?

55 **Lady Macduff** Every one that does so is a traitor, and must be hanged.

Son And must they all be hanged that swear and lie?

Lady Macduff Every one.

Son Who must hang them?

60 **Lady Macduff** Why, the honest men.

Son Then the liars and swearers are fools; for there are liars and swearers enow to beat the honest men and hang up them.

Lady Macduff Now God help thee, poor monkey! But how wilt thou do for a father?

65 **Son** If he were dead, you'ld weep for him: if you would not, it were a good sign that I should quickly have a new father.

Lady Macduff Poor prattler, how thou talk'st!

[*Enter a* **Messenger**]

Messenger Bless you, fair dame! I am not to you known,
Though in your state of honour I am perfect.
70 I doubt some danger does approach you nearly.
If you will take a homely man's advice,
Be not found here; hence, with your little ones.
To fright you thus, methinks I am too savage;
To do worse to you were fell cruelty,
75 Which is too nigh your person. Heaven preserve you!
I dare abide no longer.

[*Exit*]

Lady Macduff   Yes, he was.

Son   What is a traitor?

Lady Macduff   Why, one who swears and lies.

Son   And are all who do that traitors?

Lady Macduff   Everyone who does so is a traitor and must be hanged.

Son   And must all who swear and lie be hanged?

Lady Macduff   Every one.

Son   Who must hang them?

Lady Macduff   Why, the honest men.

Son   Then the liars and swearers are fools, for there are enough liars and swearers to beat the honest men and hang them.

Lady Macduff   Now, God help you, poor monkey! But what will you do for a father?

Son   If he truly were dead, you would weep for him. If you didn't weep for him, it would be a good sign that I should quickly get a new father.

Lady Macduff   Poor chatterbox, how you talk!

[*A* **Messenger** *enters*]

Messenger   Bless you, fair lady! You don't know me, but I am well acquainted with your noble rank. I fear some danger is soon approaching you. If you will take a plain man's advice, don't be found here. Flee with your little ones! I think it's brutal even to frighten you this way, but to let you be harmed would be savage cruelty—and that cruelty is all too near you. Heaven preserve you! I don't dare stay longer.

[*The* **Messenger** *exits*]

Lady Macduff   Whither should I fly?
I have done no harm. But I remember now
I am in this earthly world; where to do harm
80   Is often laudable, to do good sometime
Accounted dangerous folly: why then, alas,
Do I put up that womanly defence,
To say I have done no harm?

[*Enter* **Murderers**]

                  What are these faces?

85   **Murderer** Where is your husband?

Lady Macduff I hope, in no place so unsanctified
Where such as thou mayst find him.

Murderer   He's a traitor.

Son Thou liest, thou shag-haired villain.

90   **Murderer**   What, you egg!
Young fry of treachery! [*Stabs him*]

Son   He has killed me, mother:
Run away, I pray you.   [*Dies*]

[*Exit* **Lady Macduff** *crying 'murder', pursued by the*
Murderers.]

Lady Macduff   Where should I flee? I have done no harm. But I remember now that I am in this earthly world, where doing harm is often praised, and doing good is considered dangerous foolishness. Alas, then why do I make that womanish defense, saying that I've done no harm?

[*The* **Murderers** *enter*]

What are these faces?

1st Murderer   Where is your husband?

Lady Macduff   I hope in no place so unholy that someone like you might find him.

1st Murderer   He's a traitor.

Son   You lie, you hairy brute!

1st Murderer   What, you egg! Traitor's brat!

[**1st Murderer** *stabs* **Son**]

Son   He has killed me, mother. Run away, I beg you!

[**Son** *dies*]

[**Lady Macduff** *exits crying,"Murder!" pursued by the* **Murderers**]

Act IV

Scene III

England. Before the King's palace. Enter **Malcolm** *and* **Macduff.**

Malcolm Let us seek out some desolate shade, and there
Weep our sad bosoms empty.

Macduff   Let us rather
Hold fast the mortal sword, and like good men
5   Bestride our down-fall'n birthdom: each new morn
New widows howl, new orphans cry, new sorrows
Strike heaven on the face, that it resounds
As if it felt with Scotland and yelled out
Like syllable of dolour.

10 **Malcolm**   What I believe, I'll wail;
What know, believe; and what I can redress,
As I shall find the time to friend, I will.
What you have spoke, it may be so perchance.
This tyrant, whose sole name blisters our tongues,
15 Was once thought honest: you have loved him well;
He hath not touched you yet. I am young, but something
You may deserve of him through me; and wisdom
To offer up a weak, poor, innocent lamb,
T'appease an angry god.

20 **Macduff** I am not treacherous.

England. In front of King Edward the Confessor's palace.
Malcolm *and* **Macduff** *enter.*

Malcolm Let's find some dark, lonely spot, and weep there until we can weep no more.

Macduff Let's grip our deadly swords instead, and like good men defend our fallen homeland. Each new day new widows wail, new orphans cry, new sorrows strike heaven on the face. Heaven echoes as if in sympathy with Scotland and yells out similar cries of sorrow.

Malcolm I'll mourn what I believe; I'll believe what I know; and I'll correct what I can—as I find the time to do so, friend. What you have said may be true, perhaps. This tyrant, whose very name blisters our tongues, was once believed to be honest. You loved him well, and he has not injured you yet. I am young, but you might still win his favor by betraying me to him. It would be worldly-wise to offer up a weak, poor, innocent lamb to appease an angry god.

Macduff I am not treacherous.

Malcolm   But Macbeth is.
A good and virtuous nature may recoil
In an imperial charge. But I shall crave your pardon;
That which you are, my thoughts cannot transpose:
25   Angels are bright still, though the brightest fell:
Though all things foul would wear the brows of grace,
Yet grace must still look so.

Macduff   I have lost my hopes.

Malcolm   Perchance even there where I did find my doubts.
30   Why in that rawness left you wife and child,
Those precious motives, those strong knots of love,
Without leave-taking? I pray you,
Let not my jealousies be your dishonours,
But mine own safeties: you may be rightly just,
35   Whatever I shall think.

Macduff   Bleed, bleed, poor country!
Great tyranny, lay thou thy basis sure,
For goodness dares not check thee: wear thou thy wrongs,
The title is affeered! Fare thee well, lord:
40   I would not be the villain that thou think'st
For the whole space that's in the tyrant's grasp,
And the rich East to boot.

Malcolm   Be not offended:
I speak not as in absolute fear of you:
45   I think our country sinks beneath the yoke,
It weeps, it bleeds, and each new day a gash
Is added to her wounds. I think withal
There would be hands uplifted in my right;
And here from gracious England have I offer
50   Of goodly thousands. But for all this,
When I shall tread upon the tyrant's head,
Or wear it on my sword, yet my poor country
Shall have more vices than it had before,
More suffer and more sundry ways than ever,
55   By him that shall succeed.

Malcolm But Macbeth is. Even a good and virtuous nature might give way to a king's command. But I beg your pardon. My suspicions cannot change what you are. Angels are still bright even though Lucifer, the brightest angel, fell. Even though every evil thing tries to look virtuous, virtue's appearance won't change.

Macduff I have lost hope.

Malcolm Perhaps your lost hope has led to my suspicions. Why did you leave unprotected your wife and child, without saying farewell? Why leave unprotected those most precious to you, those you love most? I beg you, don't see my suspicions as dishonoring you, but only as protecting me. You may well be honorable, whatever I choose to think.

Macduff Bleed, bleed, poor country! Great tyranny, build your foundations safely, for goodness does not dare stop you. Wear what you have wrongly gained, for your title to the crown is confirmed! [*To* **Malcolm**] Farewell, lord. I would not be the criminal that you think I am for the whole country that's in the tyrant's grasp, and the rich East as well.

Malcolm Don't be offended. I don't distrust you completely. I think our country sinks into bondage. It weeps, it bleeds, and each day a new gash is added to its wounds. However, I also think that some would fight for my cause. And here I have the offer of thousands of good men from the gracious King of England. But for all that, when I have the tyrant's head under my foot or wear it on my sword, my poor country will have more vices than it had before. The man who succeeds Macbeth will make the country suffer more, and in more various ways, than ever before.

Macduff   What should he be?

Malcolm It is myself I mean: in whom I know
         All the particulars of vice so grafted
         That, when they shall be opened, black Macbeth
60   Will seem as pure as snow, and the poor state
         Esteem him as a lamb, being compared
         With my confineless harms.

Macduff   Not in the legions
         Of horrid hell can come a devil more damned
65   In evils to top Macbeth.

Malcolm   I grant him bloody,
         Luxurious, avaricious, false, deceitful,
         Sudden, malicious, smacking of every sin
         That has a name: but there's no bottom, none,
70   In my voluptuousness: your wives, your daughters,
         Your matrons and your maids, could not fill up
         The cistern of my lust, and my desire
         All continent impediments would o'erbear
         That did oppose my will. Better Macbeth,
75   Than such an one to reign.

Macduff   Boundless intemperance
         In nature is a tyranny; it hath been
         Th'untimely emptying of the happy throne,
         And fall of many kings. But fear not yet
80   To take upon you that is yours: you may
         Convey your pleasures in a spacious plenty,
         And yet seem cold, the time you may so hoodwink:
         We have willing dames enough; there cannot be
         That vulture in you, to devour so many
85   As will to greatness dedicate themselves,
         Finding it so inclined.

Malcolm   With this there grows
         In my most ill-composed affection such
         A stanchless avarice that, were I king,
90   I should cut off the nobles for their lands,

Macduff Who will he be?

Malcolm It is myself I mean. I know that the seeds of evil are so rooted in me that when they flower, black Macbeth will seem as pure as snow. The poor country will think of him as a lamb, compared to my boundless wickedness.

Macduff In all the armies of horrible hell, there can't be a devil more damned in his evils than Macbeth.

Malcolm I admit that he's murderous, lustful, greedy, false, deceitful, violent, spiteful—guilty of every sin that has a name. But there's no end, none, to my lustfulness. Your wives, your daughters, your grown women, and your young virgins could not satisfy the extent of my lust. My desire would overpower any virtuous opposition. Better that Macbeth should rule than someone like that.

Macduff Unbridled lust can tyrannize human nature. It has brought about the premature end of good rule and the fall of many kings. Still, don't be afraid to take what is yours. You can take your pleasure secretly as much as you like and still seem pure. You can deceive the world. There are enough willing women. Your desires can be so hungry that you could consume all the women who would willingly give themselves to a king, finding out his desire.

Malcolm Along with lust, an endless greed is growing in my evil nature. If I were king, I would kill nobles for their lands,

Desire his jewels and this other's house,
And my more-having would be as a sauce
To make me hunger more, that I should forge
Quarrels unjust against the good and loyal,
95   Destroying them for wealth.

Macduff   This avarice
Sticks deeper: grows with more pernicious root
Than summer-seeming lust: and it hath been
The sword of our slain kings: yet do not fear;
100   Scotland hath foisons to fill up your will
Of your mere own. All these are portable,
With other graces weighed.

Malcolm But I have none. The king-becoming graces,
As justice, verity, temp'rance, stableness,
105   Bounty, perseverance, mercy, lowliness,
Devotion, patience, courage, fortitude,
I have no relish of them, but abound
In the division of each several crime,
Acting it many ways. Nay, had I power, I should
110   Pour the sweet milk of concord into hell,
Uproot the universal peace, confound
All unity on earth.

Macduff   O Scotland! Scotland!

Malcolm If such a one be fit to govern, speak:
115   I am as I have spoken.

Macduff   Fit to govern!
No, not to live. O nation miserable!
With an untitled tyrant bloody-sceptred,
When shalt thou see thy wholesome days again,
120   Since that the truest issue of thy throne
By his own interdiction stands accurst,
And does blaspheme his breed? Thy royal father
Was a most sainted king; the queen that bore thee
Oft'ner upon her knees than on her feet,

Macduff Is Scotland still as it was?

Ross Alas, poor country, it's almost afraid to see what it's become. It cannot be called our mother, but our grave, where no one but those who know nothing ever smile. Sighs and groans and shrieks that rip the air are hardly noticed, and violent sorrow seems like a commonplace feeling. No one asks for whom a funeral bell rings, and good men's lives fade before the flowers in their caps do. They die before they have time to fall sick.

Macduff Oh, too detailed an account, but all too true!

Malcolm What's the latest grief?

Ross A report an hour old is considered stale news. Each minute gives birth to a new one.

Macduff How is my wife?

Ross Why, well.

Macduff And all my children?

Ross Well too.

Macduff The tyrant has not attacked their peace?

Ross No, they were at peace when I left them.

Macduff Don't be so stingy with your words. How goes it?

Ross When I came here to carry the news that I have sadly brought, there was a rumor that many worthy men had taken up arms. I believe this is true, because I saw the tyrant's forces on the march. Now is the time to help. [*To* **Malcolm**] If you appeared in Scotland, soldiers would spring up. Our women would fight to get rid of their terrible misfortunes.

Malcolm   Be't their comfort
215   We are coming thither: gracious England hath
      Lent us good Siward and ten thousand men;
      An older and a better soldier none
      That Christendom gives out.

Ross   Would I could answer
220   This comfort with the like! But I have words,
      That would be howled out in the desert air,
      Where hearing should not latch them.

Macduff   What concern they?
      The general cause? or is it a fee-grief
225   Due to some single breast?

Ross   No mind that's honest
      But in it shares some woe, though the main part
      Pertains to you alone.

Macduff   If it be mine,
230   Keep it not from me, quickly let me have it.

Ross Let not your ears despise my tongue for ever,
      Which shall possess them with the heaviest sound
      That ever yet they heard.

Macduff   Hum! I guess at it.

235   **Ross** Your castle is surprised; your wife and babes
      Savagely slaughtered: to relate the manner,
      Were, on the quarry of these murdered deer,
      To add the death of you.

Malcolm   Merciful heaven!
240   What, man! ne'er pull your hat upon your brows;
      Give sorrow words: the grief that does not speak
      Whispers the o'er-fraught heart and bids it break.

Macduff My children too?

Malcolm   Let them be comforted. We are coming there. The gracious King of England has lent us Siward and ten thousand men. There is not a more experienced or better soldier in Europe.

Ross   I wish I could respond with similar comfort! But I have words that should be howled out in the desert air, where no one would hear them.

Macduff   Who do these words concern? All of us? Or is it some private sorrow belonging to one person?

Ross   There's no decent person who wouldn't share it, though the main burden is yours alone.

Macduff   If it's mine, don't keep it from me. Tell me quickly.

Ross   Don't let your ears forever hate my tongue, which shall bring to them the saddest sound they've ever heard.

Macduff   Hum! I guess what it is.

Ross   Your castle was stormed, your wife and children savagely slaughtered. To tell how it was done would add you to the heap of dead, for it would kill you to hear.

Malcolm   Merciful heaven! [*To* **Macduff**] What, man, don't just pull your hat down over your eyes! Express your sorrow. Silent grief whispers to the overburdened heart and breaks it.

Macduff   [*to* **Ross**] My children, too?

Ross   Wife, children, servants, all
245   That could be found.

Macduff   And I must be from thence!
        My wife killed too?

Ross   I have said.

Malcolm   Be comforted:
250   Let's make us med'cines of our great revenge,
        To cure this deadly grief.

Macduff He has no children. All my pretty ones?
        Did you say all? O, hell-kite! All?
        What, all my pretty chickens and their dam
255   At one fell swoop?

Malcolm Dispute it like a man.

Macduff   I shall do so;
        But I must also feel it as a man:
        I cannot but remember such things were,
260   That were most precious to me. Did heaven look on,
        And would not take their part? Sinful Macduff,
        They were all struck for thee! naught that I am,
        Not for their own demerits, but for mine,
        Fell slaughter on their souls: heaven rest them now!

265 **Malcolm** Be this the whetstone of your sword: let grief
        Convert to anger; blunt not the heart, enrage it.

Macduff O, I could play the woman with mine eyes,
        And braggart with my tongue! But, gentle heavens,
        Cut short all intermission; front to front
270   Bring thou this fiend of Scotland and myself;
        Within my sword's length set him; if he 'scape,
        Heaven forgive him too!

Ross Wife, children, servants, all who could be found.

Macduff And I had to be away from there! My wife killed, too?

Ross As I told you.

Malcolm Be comforted. Let's make our great revenge the medicine that cures this terrible grief.

Macduff He has no children. All my pretty ones? Did you say all? Oh, that vulture from hell! All? What, all my pretty chickens and their mother killed in one deadly attack?

Malcolm Face it like a man.

Macduff I will; but I must also feel it like a man. I can't help remembering these things that were so precious to me. Did heaven just look on and not come to their aid? Sinful Macduff! They were all killed for you! Worthless as I am, they were slaughtered not for their misdeeds, but for mine. Heaven rest them now!

Malcolm Let this sharpen your sword. Let grief be changed to anger. Let it enrage your heart, not subdue it.

Macduff Oh, I could weep like a woman and rage like a braggart. But, gentle heavens, cut short all delay! Bring me and this Scottish fiend face-to-face. Set him within reach of my sword. If he escapes then, may heaven forgive him too!

Malcolm   This tune goes manly.
    Come, go we to the king, our power is ready,
275   Our lack is nothing but our leave. Macbeth
    Is ripe for shaking, and the powers above
    Put on their instruments. Receive what cheer you may;
    The night is long that never finds the day.

                                     [*Exeunt*]

Malcolm Spoken like a man. Come, let's go to the King. Our troops are ready. Nothing remains but to take leave of the King. Macbeth is ripe to be overthrown, and we are heaven-sent to do it. Take what comfort you can. It's a long night that doesn't end in dawn.

[*They exit*]

Comprehension **Check What You Know**

1. What is Macbeth's attitude toward the Witches in the beginning of this act? How is this different from Act 1?

2. The Witches conjure up three apparitions. What are these three apparitions, what warning does each give, and how does Macbeth react to each one?

3. What is the fourth apparition? Why is that one especially terrible to Macbeth?

4. The last king in the line holds a mirror showing more. What does this mean?

5. Compare the Macduff household and the Macbeth household. How are Lady Macduff and Lady Macbeth alike? How are they different?

6. Why does Macbeth have Macduff's wife and children killed?

7. What does Ross's speech in the beginning of Scene 2 tell you about conditions in Scotland? What justification does Ross give for Macduff's actions?

8. Scene 3 is the only scene in the entire play that does not take place in Scotland. What is the setting for this scene?

9. While Malcolm and Macduff are talking, Malcolm speaks at great length about his own vices to Macduff. What are some of the faults he names? Why does he list them for Macduff?

10. When Ross joins them later in Scene 3 and he is first asked by Macduff about his wife and children, why doesn't Ross tell him the truth?

11. What is Macduff's reaction to the news about his wife and children? What does Macduff mean when he says, "But I must also feel it as a man"?

12. What does Macduff vow to do by the end of Act 4?

©Robbie Jack/CORBIS

Activities & Role-Playing Classes or Informal Groups

Witches' Brew In the first scene the Witches put an amazing array of ingredients into their pot. List these ingredients, using the following categories: human, animal, and plant. Write down what qualities are shared by the ingredients in each category (for example, the human items are from people who are all non-Christian, which might have made them outcasts in Shakespeare's day).

Fife Castle Scene 2 is a study in contrasts. After Ross leaves the castle, Shakespeare presents a tender scene between mother and son, quickly followed by the brutal murder of the family. Role-play the scene between Lady Macduff and her son and her conversations with the Messenger, through line 83. Consider her feelings of tenderness amid her fright and confusion.

Discussion Classes or Informal Groups

1. When Macbeth confronts the Witches in Scene 1, he is a different man than he was when he first met them in Act 1. Why does he treat them so differently? What does he hope to gain from this type of behavior?

2. Discuss Macbeth's interpretations of the first three apparitions. Why does he interpret them favorably? Do you agree or disagree with his interpretation? Why? Why does he insist on seeing the fourth apparition?

3. Think about the actions of the killers of Lady Macduff, her children, and her household staff. Why do they kill these innocent people? Are there parallels to this kind of slaughter in modern times? How can such behavior be explained?

4. Ordinarily ambition is a favorable attribute. How is it corrupted by Macbeth? Is he a victim in some ways of the forces that play on him—namely, the Witches' prophecies and Lady Macbeth's influence?

Suggestions for Writing Improve Your Skills

1. Macduff left Scotland suddenly, without telling his wife and family goodbye. Write a letter that Macduff might send to his wife and children to explain his sudden departure. What reasons do you think he would have given?

2. Review Scenes 2 and 3 of this act, looking specifically for images of birds. Then, write two paragraphs that show how Shakespeare uses these images to depict Macbeth's effect on the other characters. Why do you think he might use such imagery, rather than simply stating the facts in plainer terms? In your analysis, write whether you think the use of imagery is effective, and why.

All the World's a Stage Introduction

The darkness that surrounds Macbeth has grown deeper and deeper. He has killed his king, then his friend, then the wife and children of his rival. At first he killed reluctantly, but it has gotten easier and easier. Macbeth only hinted about the plan to kill Banquo to Lady Macbeth, and his decision to kill Macduff's family is almost off-handed. And the Witches continue to promise great things for him. He has it all—or so it seems.

But tyranny rarely goes unpunished in Shakespeare's plays. Macbeth has overthrown the rightful king and driven his sons into exile. One Scots lord after another has fled to England to join forces with Malcolm, the rightful heir to the throne. Order must be restored, and the time has come for rebellion.

What's in a Name? Characters

Lady Macbeth is one of Shakespeare's most unforgettable characters. She is fierce, bold, ambitious, sensual, and willful. Her desire to be "unsexed"—to cast off any stereotyped female characteristics—so that she has the unemotional drive needed to kill King Duncan reflects the disorder in nature that has characterized the play from the beginning.

And Lady Macbeth seems to have no conscience. She doesn't brood and feel guilty. She talks as if the murder of Duncan is just a bit of housekeeping ("a little water clears us of this deed"). But as Macbeth gains more power and becomes more obsessed, Lady Macbeth has retreated from center stage. Macbeth goes to the Witches, not her, for advice and for collaboration. So even though Lady Macbeth is queen, she has far less power than she did before. In Act 5, you will learn what has become of Lady Macbeth.

COME WHAT MAY Things to Watch For

Some of the images in *Macbeth* deal with disease and cures for disease, including mental illness. King Edward of England, a good ruler who is said to be able to cure disease by his touch, is contrasted with Macbeth, whose tyranny is presented as Scotland's sickness. Malcolm's supporters see themselves as physicians who will cure their diseased homeland by bleeding it. (In Shakespeare's time, bleeding a patient was a standard remedy for a great variety of ailments.) In Act 5, you will see even more specific references to the illness that infects the country and must be cured.

The Witches' predictions in their last meeting with Macbeth seem to assure Macbeth's future. He will be killed when a woods walks to a castle and he fights a man not born of a woman. Still, in Act 5, you will see how Macbeth's attitude toward life has become more and more bleak.

One theme that has run through the play is the question of what it is to be a man. Lady Macbeth threw the question at Macbeth in Act 1, and in Act 4, when Macduff learns of the death of his wife and children, his tears are challenged by Malcolm, who says, "Why are you crying? Take it like a man and get even." Macduff replies that he must also feel his grief like a man, implying that men are entitled to cry at such a time. In Act 5, the idea of manhood is explored again.

All Our Yesterdays   Historical and Social Context

Surrounded by his enemies near the end of the play, Macbeth likens himself to a bear tied to a stake and attacked by dogs. This is an allusion to the sport of "bearbaiting," which was extremely popular in Shakespeare's England. (Queen Elizabeth herself would sometimes attend.) Bearbaiting took place twice a week, on Wednesdays and Sundays. The bear was attached by a long rope to a post fixed in the ground in the middle of a pit. Four or five large, fierce dogs, such as mastiffs, were let into the pit and attacked the bear.

The Play's the Thing   Staging

Shakespeare wrote his most powerful male roles for the actor Richard Burbage, the first great English actor. Burbage must also have been a skilled swordsman, given the demands of the last scenes of the play. As the rebellion comes to Macbeth, he ultimately must face his most formidable foe in a swordfight. Because people in the Renaissance were knowledgeable about swordplay, any actor had to be very good.

My Words Fly Up   Language

Several of Shakespeare's most famous soliloquies are in Act 5 of *Macbeth*. One begins "I have lived long enough: my way of life / Is fall'n into the sere, the yellow leaf" (5, 3, 25–31). Another begins "To-morrow, and to-morrow, and to-morrow" (5, 5, 21–30). Some commentators say that these speeches could only have been written by a mature playwright. Others say that the speeches were written by a playwright frightened by his vision of disorder in a country. Still others say that they were written by someone who had contemplated how badly people can act when tempted by their most cherished dream. As you read through this act, see what you think.

In one of Macbeth's speeches, he compares life with a play. In this speech, a *player* is an actor. In another place, Macbeth talks about acting like a Roman. This is a reference to the belief that when a general in Rome knew he was about to lose a battle, he would commit suicide by falling on his sword.

Act V

Scene I

Dunsinane. A room in the castle. Enter a **Doctor of Physic,** *and a* **Waiting Gentlewoman.**

Doctor I have two nights watched with you, but can perceive no truth in your report. When was it she last walked?

Gentlewoman Since his majesty went into the field, I have seen her rise from her bed, throw her night-gown upon her,
5 unlock her closet, take forth paper, fold it, write upon't, read it, afterwards seal it, and again return to bed; yet all this while in a most fast sleep.

Doctor A great perturbation in nature, to receive at once the benefit of sleep and do the effects of watching! In this
10 slumbery agitation, besides her walking and other actual performances, what, at any time, have you heard her say?

Gentlewoman That, sir, which I will not report after her.

Doctor You may to me, and 'tis most meet you should.

Gentlewoman Neither to you nor any one, having no witness
15 to confirm my speech.

[*Enter* **Lady Macbeth,** *with a taper*]

Lo you, here she comes! This is her very guise, and upon my life fast asleep. Observe her, stand close.

Doctor How came she by that light?

204

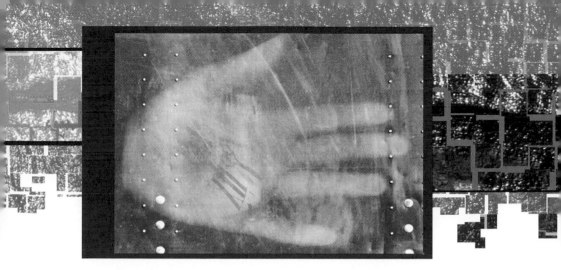

A room in Macbeth's castle at Dunsinane. A **Doctor** *and a*
Lady-in-Waiting *enter.*

Doctor I have stood watch with you for two nights, but I can
see no truth in your report. When was it that she last walked?

Lady-in-Waiting Ever since His Majesty went to war, I have
seen her rise from her bed, put on her nightgown, unlock her
closet, take a paper out of it, fold it, write on it, read it, then
seal it up, and return to bed again. All the time she did this
she was fast asleep.

Doctor A great disorder in nature, to have the benefit of sleep
and act as if wide awake at the same time! In this restless
slumber, besides her walking and other actual deeds, what,
at any time, have you heard her say?

Lady-in-Waiting What she's said I will not repeat about her.

Doctor You may tell me, and it's most suitable that you should.

Lady-in-Waiting Neither to you nor to anyone else, since I have
no witness to confirm what I say.

[**Lady Macbeth** *enters, carrying a candle*]

Look, here she comes! This is her usual manner, and I'll
swear she's fast asleep. Watch her. Stay hidden.

[*They stand aside*]

Doctor How did she get the light?

Gentlewoman Why, it stood by her: she has light by her
20   continually, 'tis her command.

Doctor You see, her eyes are open.

Gentlewoman Ay, but their sense are shut.

Doctor What is it she does now? Look, how she rubs her
      hands.

25 **Gentlewoman** It is an accustomed action with her, to seem
      thus washing her hands: I have known her continue in this a
      quarter of an hour.

Lady Macbeth Yet here's a spot.

Doctor Hark, she speaks! I will set down what comes from
30   her, to satisfy my remembrance the more strongly.

Lady Macbeth Out, damned spot! out, I say! One: two: why,
      then 'tis time to do't. Hell is murky! Fie, my lord, fie! a
      soldier, and afeard? What need we fear who knows it, when
      none can call our power to accompt? Yet who would have
35   thought the old man to have had so much blood in him?

Doctor Do you mark that?

Lady Macbeth The Thane of Fife had a wife; where is she
      now? What, will these hands ne'er be clean? No more o'that,
      my lord, no more o'that: you mar all with this starting.

40 **Doctor** Go to, go to; you have known what you should not.

Gentlewoman She has spoke what she should not, I am sure
      of that: heaven knows what she has known.

Lady Macbeth Here's the smell of the blood still: all the
      perfumes of Arabia will not sweeten this little hand. Oh! oh!
45   oh!

Doctor What a sigh is there! The heart is sorely charged.

Gentlewoman I would not have such a heart in my bosom, for
      the dignity of the whole body.

Lady-in-Waiting Why, it was by her bed. She has light by her always. It's her orders.

Doctor You see her eyes are open.

Lady-in-Waiting Yes, but they see nothing.

Doctor What is she doing now? Look how she rubs her hands.

Lady-in-Waiting It is her habit to seem to be washing her hands. I have known her to keep doing this for a quarter of an hour.

Lady Macbeth Yet here's a spot.

Doctor Listen, she speaks. I will write down what she says, to further support my memory.

Lady Macbeth Out, damned spot! Out, I say! One. Two. Why then, it's time to do it. Hell is murky. For shame, my lord, for shame—a soldier and afraid? Why should we fear who knows it, when no one can challenge our authority? Yet who would have thought the old man would have had so much blood in him?

Doctor Did you hear that?

Lady Macbeth The Thane of Fife had a wife. Where is she now? What, will these hands never be clean? No more of that, my lord, no more of that. You'll ruin everything with your panicking.

Doctor [*To* **Lady-in-Waiting**] Now, now. You have learned what you shouldn't.

Lady-in-Waiting She has spoken what she shouldn't, I'm sure of that. Heaven knows what she has known.

Lady Macbeth The smell of blood is still here. All the perfumes of Arabia will not sweeten this little hand. Oh, oh, oh!

Doctor What a sigh that was! Her heart is heavy-burdened.

Lady-in-Waiting I would not have such a heart in my breast even to be queen.

Doctor Well, well, well, –

50 **Gentlewoman** Pray God it be, sir.

Doctor This disease is beyond my practice: yet I have known
    those which have walked in their sleep who have died holily
    in their beds.

Lady Macbeth Wash your hands, put on your night-gown,
55   look not so pale: I tell you yet again, Banquo's buried; he
    cannot come out on's grave.

Doctor Even so?

Lady Macbeth To bed, to bed: there's knocking at the gate:
    come, come, come, come, give me your hand: what's done,
60   cannot be undone: to bed, to bed, to bed.

                                            [*Exit*]

Doctor Will she go now to bed?

Gentlewoman Directly.

Doctor Foul whisp'rings are abroad: unnatural deeds
    Do breed unnatural troubles: infected minds
65   To their deaf pillows will discharge their secrets:
    More needs she the divine than the physician:
    God, God forgive us all! Look after her,
    Remove from her the means of all annoyance,
    And still keep eyes upon her. So, good night:
70   My mind she has mated and amazed my sight:
    I think, but dare not speak.

Gentlewoman   Good night, good doctor.

                                            [*Exeunt*]

Doctor Well, well, well.

Lady-in-Waiting Pray God it be well, sir.

Doctor This disease is beyond my medical skill. Yet I have known those that have walked in their sleep who died holy deaths in their beds.

Lady Macbeth Wash your hands. Put on your nightgown. Don't look so pale! I tell you once again—Banquo's buried. He cannot come out of his grave.

Doctor So that's what happened?

Lady Macbeth To bed, to bed! There's a knocking at the gate. Come, come, come, come. Give me your hand. What's done cannot be undone. To bed, to bed, to bed!

[**Lady Macbeth** *leaves*]

Doctor Will she go to bed now?

Lady-in-Waiting Right away.

Doctor There are evil rumors circulating. Unnatural deeds will breed unnatural troubles. Sick minds will confide their secrets to their deaf pillows. She needs a priest more than a doctor. God, God forgive us all! Look after her. Take away anything with which she can hurt herself. And continue to keep an eye on her. So, good night. She has bewildered my mind and amazed my sight. I dare not speak my thoughts.

Lady-in-Waiting Good night, good doctor.

[*They leave*]

Act V

Scene II

The country near Dunsinane. Drum and colours. Enter
Menteith, Caithness, Angus, Lennox, *and* **Soldiers.**

Menteith The English power is near, led on by Malcolm,
His uncle Siward and the good Macduff.
Revenges burn in them: for their dear causes
Would to the bleeding and the grim alarm
5   Excite the mortified man.

Angus   Near Birnam wood
Shall we meet them, and that way are they coming.

Caithness Who knows if Donalbain be with his brother?

Lennox For certain, sir, he is not: I have a file
10   Of all the gentry: there is Siward's son,
And many unrough youths, that even now
Protest their first of manhood.

Menteith   What does the tyrant?

Caithness Great Dunsinane he strongly fortifies:
15   Some say he's mad; others, that lesser hate him,
Do call it valiant fury: but, for certain,
He cannot buckle his distempered cause
Within the belt of rule.

The country near Dunsinane. Drums beat and flags fly.
Menteith, Caithness, Angus, Lennox, *and* **Soldiers** *enter.*

Menteith The English army is nearby, led by Malcolm, his uncle Siward, and the good Macduff. Revenge burns in them, for the terrible wrongs done them would cause even a dead man to answer the grim and bloody call to battle.

Angus We shall meet them near Birnam Wood. They are coming that way.

Caithness Does anyone know if Donalbain is with his brother?

Lennox It is certain, sir, that he isn't. I have a list of all the nobles. There is Siward's son, and many young men that are showing their manhood in public for the first time.

Menteith What is the tyrant doing?

Caithness He has strongly fortified great Dunsinane. Some say he's gone mad. Others who hate him less call it a brave fury. One thing is certain: he has lost all self-control.

Angus   Now does he feel
20   His secret murders sticking on his hands;
     Now minutely revolts upbraid his faith-breach;
     Those he commands move only in command,
     Nothing in love: now does he feel his title
     Hang loose about him, like a giant's robe
25   Upon a dwarfish thief.

Menteith   Who then shall blame
     His pestered senses to recoil and start,
     When all that is within him does condemn
     Itself for being there?

30 **Caithness**   Well, march we on,
     To give obedience where 'tis truly owed:
     Meet we the med'cine of the sickly weal,
     And with him pour we, in our country's purge,
     Each drop of us.

35 **Lennox**   Or so much as it needs
     To dew the sovereign flower and drown the weeds.
     Make we our march towards Birnam.

                    [*Exeunt, marching*]

Angus Now he feels his secret murders sticking to his hands. Now his treason is attacked every minute by rebels. Those he commands obey only by fear, not by love. Now he feels his royal title is too big for him, like a giant's robe on a dwarfish thief.

Menteith Who could blame his tormented feelings of disgust and fear, when the spirit within him must condemn itself for being there?

Caithness Well, let's march on to give obedience where it's properly due. Let us meet Malcolm, a doctor for our sick country, and with him we'll shed our blood to rid our country of this disease.

Lennox Or as much as is needed to make our true king flower and drown the weeds. Let's march toward Birnam.

[*They march off*]

Act V

Scene III

Dunsinane. A court in the castle. Enter **Macbeth, Doctor,**
and **Attendants.**

Macbeth Bring me no more reports, let them fly all:
    Till Birnam wood remove to Dunsinane
    I cannot taint with fear. What's the boy Malcolm?
    Was he not born of woman? The spirits that know
5   All mortal consequence have pronounced me thus:
    'Fear not, Macbeth, no man that's born of woman
    Shall e'er have power upon thee'. Then fly, false thanes,
    And mingle with the English epicures:
    The mind I sway by and the heart I bear
10   Shall never sag with doubt nor shake with fear.

    [*Enter a* **Servant**]

    The devil damn thee black, thou cream-faced loon!
    Where got'st thou that goose look?

Servant There is ten thousand –

Macbeth   Geese, villain?

15 **Servant**   Soldiers, sir.

Macbeth Go prick thy face and over-red thy fear,
    Thou lily-livered boy. What soldiers, patch?
    Death of thy soul! those linen cheeks of thine
    Are counsellors to fear. What soldiers, whey-face?

Macbeth's castle at Dunsinane. **Macbeth, Doctor,** *and* **Attendants** *enter.*

Macbeth Bring me no more reports. Let all of my thanes flee! Till Birnam Wood comes to Dunsinane, I have no fear. Who is this boy Malcolm? Was he not born of woman? The spirits that know everything that will happen have told me this: "Fear not, Macbeth. No man that's born of woman shall ever have power over you." Flee then, false thanes, and join the English weaklings. The mind that rules me and the heart within me shall never give way to doubt or shake with fear.

[*A* **Servant** *enters*]

May the devil turn you black, you pale-faced fool! Where did you get that goose look?

Servant There are ten thousand—

Macbeth Geese, villain?

Servant Soldiers, sir.

Macbeth Go pinch some red into your face and mask your fear, you lily-livered boy. What soldiers, fool? Damn you! Those white cheeks of yours teach others to fear. What soldiers, milksop?

20 **Servant**   The English force, so please you.

Macbeth   Take thy face hence.

[*Exit* **Servant**]

Seton! – I am sick at heart
When I behold – Seton, I say! – This push
Will cheer me ever, or disseat me now.
25   I have lived long enough: my way of life
Is fall'n into the sere, the yellow leaf,
And that which should accompany old age,
As honour, love, obedience, troops of friends,
I must not look to have; but, in their stead,
30   Curses, not loud but deep, mouth-honour, breath
Which the poor heart would fain deny and dare not.
Seton!
[*Enter* **Seton**]

Seton   What is your gracious pleasure?

Macbeth   What news more?

35 **Seton**   All is confirmed, my lord, which was reported.

Macbeth   I'll fight, till from my bones my flesh be hacked.
Give me my armour.

Seton   'Tis not needed yet.

Macbeth   I'll put it on.
40   Send out more horses, skirr the country round,
Hang those talk of fear. Give me mine armour.
How goes your patient, Doctor?

Doctor   Not so sick, my lord,
As she is troubled with thick-coming fancies,
45   That keep her from her rest.

Macbeth   Cure her of that:
Canst thou not minister to a mind diseased,

Servant   The English army, so please you.

Macbeth   Take your face away. [*The* **Servant** *leaves*] Seton!—
[*To himself*] I am sick at heart when I behold—Seton, I
say!—This fight will keep me on the throne for good or I'll be
lost. I have lived long enough. My life has reached its
withered, yellow autumn. And that which should accompany
old age—such as honor, love, obedience, troops of friends—I
must not expect to have; but instead, I'll have curses—not
spoken aloud, but heartfelt—and lip-service, which the weak
heart would like to deny but dares not. Seton!

[**Seton** *enters*]

Seton   What is your majesty's pleasure?

Macbeth   What's the latest news?

Seton   That which was reported has been confirmed, my lord.

Macbeth   I'll fight till my flesh is hacked from my bones. Give
me my armor.

Seton   It's not needed yet.

Macbeth   I'll put it on. Send out more horsemen. Scour the
surrounding country. Hang anyone who talks of fear. Give me
my armor. [*To the* **Doctor**] How is your patient, Doctor?

Doctor   She is not so much sick, my lord, as she is troubled by
frequent fantasies that keep her from resting.

Macbeth   Cure her of that. Can't you help a sick mind? Pluck
out a sorrow rooted in the memory? Erase the troubles

Pluck from the memory a rooted sorrow,
Raze out the written troubles of the brain,
50 And with some sweet oblivious antidote
Cleanse the stuffed bosom of that perilous stuff
Which weighs upon the heart?

Doctor   Therein the patient
Must minister to himself.

55 **Macbeth**   Throw physic to the dogs, I'll none of it.
Come, put mine armour on; give me my staff;
Seton, send out; Doctor, the thanes fly from me;
Come, sir, dispatch. – If thou couldst, Doctor, cast
The water of my land, find her disease,
60 And purge it to a sound and pristine health,
I would applaud thee to the very echo
That should applaud again. – Pull't off, I say. –
What rhubarb, senna, or what purgative drug,
Would scour these English hence? Hear'st thou of them?

65 **Doctor**   Ay, my good lord; your royal preparation
Makes us hear something.

Macbeth   Bring it after me.
I will not be afraid of death and bane
Till Birnam forest come to Dunsinane.

[*Exeunt* **Macbeth** *and* **Seton**]

70 **Doctor**   Were I from Dunsinane away and clear,
Profit again should hardly draw me here.

[*Exit*]

written on the brain? Cleanse the heart of its dangerous burdens with some drug that causes sweet forgetfulness?

Doctor   In these things, the patient must help himself.

Macbeth   Throw medicine to the dogs! I don't want it. Come, put my armor on. Give me my lance. [*The* **Attendants** *arm him. To* **Seton**] Seton, send out more men. [*To* **Doctor**] Doctor, my thanes abandon me. [*To* **Seton**] Come, sir, hurry.—[*To* **Doctor**] If you could examine my country, Doctor, find out her disease, and make her as sound and healthy as she once was, I would loudly applaud you, over and over.— [*To* **Seton**] Take it off, I tell you.—[*To* **Doctor**] What drugs would cleanse us of these English? Have you heard of them?

Doctor   Yes, my good lord. Your majesty's preparation makes us aware of them.

Macbeth   [*To* **Seton**] Follow me with it. [*To himself*] I will not fear death or doom till Birnam Forest comes to Dunsinane.

[*All leave but the* **Doctor**]

Doctor   If I could get safely away from Dunsinane, money would not tempt me back.

[*The* **Doctor** *leaves*]

Act V

Scene IV

Country near Birnam Wood. Drum and colours. Enter
**Malcolm, Siward, Macduff, Siward's son, Menteith,
Caithness, Angus, Lennox, Ross,** *and* **Soldiers,** *marching.*

Malcolm   Cousins, I hope, the days are near at hand
   That chambers will be safe.

Menteith   We doubt it nothing.

Siward   What wood is this before us?

5 **Menteith**   The wood of Birnam.

Malcolm   Let every soldier hew him down a bough,
   And bear't before him: thereby shall we shadow
   The numbers of our host, and make discovery
   Err in report of us.

10 **Soldier**   It shall be done.

Siward   We learn no other but the confident tyrant
   Keeps still in Dunsinane, and will endure
   Our setting down before't.

Malcolm   'Tis his main hope:
15   For where there is advantage to be gone,
   Both more and less have given him the revolt,
   And none serve with him but constrained things
   Whose hearts are absent too.

Country near Birnam Wood. Drums beat and flags fly.
Malcolm, Siward, Macduff, Siward's Son, Menteith, Caithness, Angus, Lennox, Ross, *and some* **Soldiers** *enter, marching.*

Malcolm Cousins, I hope the time is close when we will sleep safe in our homes.

Menteith We do not doubt it.

Siward What forest is this in front of us?

Menteith Birnam Wood.

Malcolm Have every soldier cut down a branch and carry it in front of him. In that way we will conceal the size of our army and make scouts give false reports of us.

Soldier It shall be done.

Siward We hear nothing but that the confident tyrant still remains in his castle at Dunsinane and will not try to prevent us from laying siege to it.

Malcolm It's his best hope. For whenever there has been opportunity, both officers and men have deserted him. None serve with him but those who are forced to, and they have no loyalty.

Macduff   Let our just censures
20 Attend the true event, and put we on
 Industrious soldiership.

Siward   The time approaches,
 That will with due decision make us know
 What we shall say we have and what we owe.
25 Thoughts speculative their unsure hopes relate,
 But certain issue strokes must arbitrate:
 Towards which advance the war.

         [*Exeunt, marching*]

Macduff Let's wait to pass judgment until the outcome is clear. Meanwhile, let's be careful soldiers.

Siward The time is near when we will know the difference between what we think we can achieve and what we really can. Speculation only shows what we hope; battle is the final judge. Have the army advance.

[*They leave, marching*]

Act V

Scene V

Dunsinane. The court of the castle as before. Enter **Macbeth,**
Seton, *and* **Soldiers** *with drum and colours.*

Macbeth Hang out our banners on the outward walls;
The cry is still 'They come': our castle's strength
Will laugh a siege to scorn: here let them lie
Till famine and the ague eat them up:
5   Were they not forced with those that should be ours,
We might have met them dareful, beard to beard,
And beat them backward home.

[*A cry of women within*]

What is that noise?

Seton It is the cry of women, my good lord.

[*Exit*]

10 **Macbeth** I have almost forgot the taste of fears:
The time has been, my senses would have cooled
To hear a night-shriek, and my fell of hair
Would at a dismal treatise rouse and stir
As life were in't: I have supped full with horrors;
15   Direness, familiar to my slaughterous thoughts,
Cannot once start me.

[*Re-enter* **Seton**]

Wherefore was that cry?

Macbeth's castle at Dunsinane. **Macbeth, Seton,** *and some* **Soldiers** *enter, with drums beating and flags flying.*

Macbeth Hang out our banners on the outer walls. The cry remains, "They're coming!" Our castle's strength will make a siege laughable. Let the enemy stay here till famine and fever destroy them. If they were not reinforced with those who deserted us, we might have met them in open battle, face to face, and beat them back to their homes. [*Women cry offstage*] What is that noise?

Seton It is women crying, my good lord.

[**Seton** *goes to the door*]

Macbeth I have almost forgotten the taste of fear. There was a time when a shriek in the night would turn me cold, and a frightening story would make my hair stand on end as if it were alive. I have had my fill of horrors. Dreadful things, familiar to my murderous thoughts, can't frighten me at all. [**Seton** *returns*] What was the reason for that cry?

Seton The queen, my lord, is dead.

Macbeth She should have died hereafter;
20   There would have been a time for such a word.
      To-morrow, and to-morrow, and to-morrow,
      Creeps in this petty pace from day to day,
      To the last syllable of recorded time;
      And all our yesterdays have lighted fools
25   The way to dusty death. Out, out, brief candle!
      Life's but a walking shadow, a poor player
      That struts and frets his hour upon the stage,
      And then is heard no more: it is a tale
      Told by an idiot, full of sound and fury,
30   Signifying nothing.

      [*Enter a* **Messenger**]

      Thou com'st to use thy tongue; thy story quickly.

Messenger Gracious my lord,
      I should report that which I say I saw,
      But know not how to do't.

35 **Macbeth**   Well, say, sir.

Messenger As I did stand my watch upon the hill,
      I looked toward Birnam, and anon, methought
      The wood began to move.

Macbeth   Liar and slave!

40 **Messenger** Let me endure your wrath, if't be not so:
      Within this three mile may you see it coming.
      I say, a moving grove.

Macbeth   If thou speak'st false,
      Upon the next tree shalt thou hang alive,
45   Till famine cling thee: if thy speech be sooth,

226

Seton The Queen, my lord, is dead.

Macbeth She would have died sometime; someday the word
would have arrived. Tomorrow, and tomorrow, and
tomorrow creeps in this slow pace from day to day to the
end of time. And all of our yesterdays are just a light to guide
fools to their graves. Out, out, brief candle! Life is but a
walking shadow, a wretched actor that struts and worries for
a short time on the stage and then is gone. It is a tale told by
an idiot, full of sound and fury, but signifying nothing.

[*A* **Messenger** *enters*]

You come to tell me something. Your report quickly.

Messenger My gracious lord, I must report what I believe I
saw, but don't know how to do it.

Macbeth Well, speak, sir.

Messenger As I was standing my watch on the hill, I looked
toward Birnam, and soon, I thought, the wood began to
move.

Macbeth Liar and slave!

Messenger Let me endure your anger if this isn't true. You can
see it coming not three miles away; I tell you, a moving
grove.

Macbeth If you are speaking falsely, I shall hang you alive on
the next tree till hunger makes you shrivel. If your words are

I care not if thou dost for me as much.
I pull in resolution, and begin
To doubt th'equivocation of the fiend.
That lies like truth: 'Fear not, till Birnam wood
50 Do come to Dunsinane'; and now a wood
Comes toward Dunsinane. Arm, arm, and out!
If this which he avouches does appear,
There is nor flying hence nor tarrying here.
I 'gin to be aweary of the sun,
55 And wish th'estate o'th' world were now undone.
Ring the alarum bell! Blow, wind! come, wrack!
At least we'll die with harness on our back.

[Exeunt]

true, I don't care if you do the same thing to me. [*To himself*] I begin to lose my confident determination and to doubt the double meanings of the devil who makes lies sound like truth. "Fear not, till Birnam Wood comes to Dunsinane," and now a wood comes toward Dunsinane. [*To* **Soldiers**] To arms, to arms, and to the battlefield! [*To himself*] If what he swears is true, there is no fleeing or staying here. I begin to be weary of the sun, and wish the order of the world would collapse. [*To* **Soldiers**] Ring the alarm bell! Blow wind, come ruin, at least we'll die fighting.

[*They leave*]

Act V

Scene VI

Dunsinane. Before the castle gate. Drum and colours. Enter
Malcolm, Siward, Macduff, *and their army, with boughs.*

Malcolm   Now near enough: your leavy screens throw down,
And show like those you are. You, worthy uncle,
Shall with my cousin your right-noble son
Lead our first battle: worthy Macduff and we
5   Shall take upon's what else remains to do,
According to our order.

Siward   Fare you well.
Do we but find the tyrant's power to-night,
Let us be beaten, if we cannot fight.

10   **Macduff**   Make all our trumpets speak; give them all breath,
Those clamorous harbingers of blood and death.

[*Exeunt*]

Outside Macbeth's castle. Drums are beating and flags are flying. Enter **Malcolm, Siward, Macduff,** *and their army, carrying branches.*

Malcolm We're near enough now. Throw down the branches that screen you and show yourselves as you are. You, worthy uncle, and my cousin, your very noble son, shall lead our first attack. According to our plan, worthy Macduff and I will take care of whatever else remains to be done.

Siward Farewell. If we find the tyrant's army tonight, may we be beaten if we don't fight hard.

Macduff Sound all our trumpets! Blow them all, those clamorous heralds of blood and death.

[*They leave. The trumpet calls continue*]

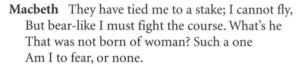

Act V

Scene VII

Another part of the field

Macbeth They have tied me to a stake; I cannot fly,
But bear-like I must fight the course. What's he
That was not born of woman? Such a one
Am I to fear, or none.

[*Enter* **Young Siward**]

5 **Young Siward** What is thy name?

Macbeth   Thou'lt be afraid to hear it.

Young Siward No; though thou call'st thyself a hotter name
Than any is in hell.

Macbeth   My name's Macbeth.

10 **Young Siward** The devil himself could not pronounce a title
More hateful to mine ear.

Macbeth   No, nor more fearful;

Young Siward Thou liest, abhorred tyrant; with my sword
I'll prove the lie thou speak'st.

[*They fight, and* **Young Siward** *is slain*]

Outside Macbeth's castle. **Macbeth** *enters.*

Macbeth   They have tied me to a stake. I cannot flee, but like a bear I must fight to the end. Who is the man that was not born of woman? I am to fear such a man, or no one.

[**Young Siward** *enters*]

Young Siward   What is your name?

Macbeth   You will be afraid to hear it.

Young Siward   No, even if you call yourself a hotter name than any that is in hell.

Macbeth   My name's Macbeth.

Young Siward   The devil himself could not speak a name more hateful to my ear.

Macbeth   No, nor more fearful.

Young Siward   You lie, hated tyrant. I'll prove that you lie with my sword!

[*They fight.* **Young Siward** *is killed*]

15 **Macbeth**   Thou wast born of woman.
      But swords I smile at, weapons laugh to scorn,
      Brandished by man that's of a woman born.

[*Alarums. Enter* **Macduff**]

Macduff That way the noise is. Tyrant, show thy face!
      If thou be'est slain and with no stroke of mine,
20   My wife and children's ghosts will haunt me still.
      I cannot strike at wretched kerns, whose arms
      Are hired to bear their staves; either thou, Macbeth,
      Or else my sword with an unbattered edge
      I sheathe again undeeded. There thou shouldst be;
25   By this great clatter, one of greatest note
      Seems bruited. Let me find him, fortune!
      And more I beg not.

[**Malcolm** *and* **Siward** *come up*]

Siward This way, my lord; the castle's gently rendered:
      The tyrant's people on both sides do fight,
30   The noble thanes do bravely in the war,
      The day almost itself professes yours,
      And little is to do.

Malcolm   We have met with foes
      That strike beside us.

35 **Siward**   Enter, sir, the castle.

                                      [*Exeunt*]

[**Macbeth** *returns*]

Macbeth Why should I play the Roman fool, and die
      On mine own sword? whiles I see lives, the gashes
      Do better upon them.

Macbeth   You were born of woman. But I smile at swords and laugh with scorn at weapons brandished by a man that is born of woman.

[**Macbeth** *leaves*]

[*Trumpets sound.* **Macduff** *enters*]

Macduff   The noise is that way. Tyrant, show your face! If you've been killed, and not by my sword, the ghosts of my wife and children will always haunt me. I cannot fight with mere foot soldiers, who are hired to fight. Either I find you, Macbeth, or else I sheathe my sword again, unmarked and unused. You should be over there, where the great noise seems to announce someone of the highest rank. Let me find him, Fortune, and I beg for nothing more.

[*He leaves. Trumpets sound.* **Malcolm** *and* **Siward** *enter*]

Siward   This way, my lord. The castle surrendered without a fight. The tyrant's men fight on both sides. Your nobles fight bravely in battle, victory is almost yours, and there is little left to do.

Malcolm   I have fought with enemies that have fought beside me.

Siward   Enter the castle, sir.

[*They leave. Trumpets sound.* **Macbeth** *enters*]

Macbeth   Why should I act like a foolish Roman and die on my own sword? While I see living enemies, the wounds are better on them.

[*Enter* **Macduff**]

Macduff   Turn, hell-hound, turn.

40 **Macbeth**   Of all men else I have avoided thee:
But get thee back, my soul is too much charged
With blood of thine already.

Macduff   I have no words:
My voice is in my sword, thou bloodier villain
45 Than terms can give thee out!

[*They fight*]

Macbeth   Thou losest labour.
As easy mayst thou the intrenchant air
With thy keen sword impress as make me bleed:
Let fall thy blade on vulnerable crests,
50 I bear a charmed life, which must not yield
To one of woman born.

Macduff   Despair thy charm,
And let the angel whom thou still hast served
Tell thee, Macduff was from his mother's womb
55 Untimely ripped.

Macbeth   Accursed be that tongue that tells me so,
For it hath cowed my better part of man!
And be these juggling fiends no more believed,
That palter with us in a double sense,
60 That keep the word of promise to our ear,
And break it to our hope. I'll not fight with thee.

Macduff   Then yield thee, coward,
And live to be the show and gaze o'th' time.
We'll have thee, as our rarer monsters are,
65 Painted upon a pole, and underwrit,
'Here may you see the tyrant'.

[**Macduff** *enters*]

Macduff Turn, hellhound, turn!

Macbeth I have avoided you more than all the others. I am already too guilty of shedding your family's blood.

Macduff I have nothing to say. My sword will speak for me, you bloodier villain than mere words can say.

[*They fight. Trumpets sound*]

Macbeth You're wasting effort. You can as easily wound the air with your sharp sword as make me bleed. Let your blade fall on heads you can wound. I have a charmed life and cannot be taken by one born of a woman.

Macduff Lose hope in your magic spell, and let the evil angel you serve tell you that Macduff was prematurely ripped from his mother's womb.

Macbeth Cursed be the tongue that tells me this, for it has robbed me of my manly courage! And no more let these deceiving devils be believed. They speak to us with a double meaning, keeping the words of the promise we heard but denying what we hoped for. I will not fight with you.

Macduff Then surrender, coward, and live to be put on display. We'll put a painted image of you on a pole, the way we do with our rarer monsters. And written underneath will be, "Here you may see the tyrant."

Macbeth   I will not yield,
    To kiss the ground before young Malcolm's feet,
    And to be baited with the rabble's curse.
70 Though Birnam wood be come to Dunsinane,
    And thou opposed, being of no woman born,
    Yet I will try the last. Before my body
    I throw my warlike shield: lay on, Macduff,
    And damned be him that first cries, 'Hold, enough.'

                    [*Exeunt, fighting*]

Retreat and flourish. Enter, with drum and colours,
Malcolm, Siward, Ross, Thanes *and* **Soldiers.**

75 **Malcolm** I would the friends we miss were safe arrived.

Siward Some must go off: and yet, by these I see,
    So great a day as this is cheaply bought.

Malcolm Macduff is missing, and your noble son.

Ross Your son, my lord, has paid a soldier's debt:
80 He only lived but till he was a man,
    The which no sooner had his prowess confirmed
    In the unshrinking station where he fought,
    But like a man he died.

Siward   Then he is dead?

85 **Ross** Ay, and brought off the field: your cause of sorrow
    Must not be measured by his worth, for then
    It hath no end.

Siward   Had he his hurts before?

Ross Ay, on the front.

90 **Siward**   Why then, God's soldier be he!
    Had I as many sons as I have hairs,

Macbeth I will not surrender to kiss the ground before young Malcolm's feet and be tormented by jeering crowds. Though Birnam Wood is come to Dunsinane, and I'm facing you, who are not of woman born, yet I will fight to the end. I put my warrior's shield in front of my body. Strike, Macduff, and let him be damned that cries first, "Stop, enough!"

[*They leave fighting. Trumpets sound*]

[*A trumpet sounds, ending the fighting.* **Malcolm, Siward, Ross, Thanes,** *and* **Soldiers** *enter, with drums beating and flags flying*]

Malcolm I wish our missing friends were safely here.

Siward Some must be dead. And yet, judging by those I see here, this great victory was won cheaply.

Malcolm Macduff is missing, and your noble son.

Ross Your son, my lord, died like a soldier. He only lived until he reached manhood. No sooner had he shown that valor by holding his ground than he died like a man.

Siward Then he is dead?

Ross Yes, and carried off the battlefield. Your grief must not be equal to his worth, for then it would have no end.

Siward Were his wounds in front?

Ross Yes, in front.

Siward Why then, he's God's soldier now! If I had as many sons as I have hairs, I could not wish any of them a better

I would not wish them to a fairer death:
And so his knell is knolled.

Malcolm   He's worth more sorrow,
95   And that I'll spend for him.

Siward   He's worth no more.
They say he parted well and paid his score:
And so God be with him! Here comes newer comfort.

[*Re-enter* **Macduff,** *with* **Macbeth**'s *head*]

Macduff Hail, king! for so thou art. Behold where stands
100   Th'usurper's cursed head: the time is free:
I see thee compassed with thy kingdom's pearl,
That speak my salutation in their minds;
Whose voice I desire aloud with mine:
Hail, king of Scotland!

105 **All**   Hail, king of Scotland!

Malcolm We shall not spend a large expense of time
Before we reckon with your several loves,
And make us even with you. My thanes and kinsmen,
Henceforth be earls, the first that ever Scotland
110   In such an honour named. What's more to do,
Which would be planted newly with the time,
As calling home our exiled friends abroad
That fled the snares of watchful tyranny,
Producing forth the cruel ministers
115   Of this dead butcher and his fiend-like queen,
Who, as 'tis thought, by self and violent hands
Took off her life; this, and what needful else
That calls upon us, by the grace of Grace
We will perform in measure, time, and place:
120   So thanks to all at once, and to each one,
Whom we invite to see us crowned at Scone.

[*Exeunt*]

death. And so, his funeral bell is rung.

Malcolm He's worth more sorrow, and I will give it to him.

Siward He's worth no more. They say he died well and did his duty. And so, God be with him! Here comes newer comfort.

[**Macduff** *enters carrying Macbeth's head on a pole*]

Macduff Hail king! For that is what you are. See where the usurper's cursed head stands. Our time is free of tyranny. I see you surrounded by the finest men in your kingdom. They speak my greeting in their minds. I want their voices to join aloud with mine: Hail, King of Scotland!

All Hail, King of Scotland!

[*Trumpets sound*]

Malcolm We shall not waste any time before repaying each of you for your loyalty. My thanes and kinsmen, from now on you are all earls, the first ever given such an honor in Scotland. There are other things that we will do to mark the beginning of this new era. We will call home from abroad our exiled friends that fled from the plots of the suspicious tyrant. We will bring to trial the cruel agents of this dead butcher and his fiendish queen—who, it is said, turned her violence on herself and took her own life. These things, and whatever else is necessary, we will, by the grace of God, perform at the proper time and place. So, thanks to each and every one of you. We invite you to see us crowned at Scone.

[*Trumpets sound as they all leave*]

Comprehension **Check What You Know**

1. What does the sleepwalking scene tell you about Lady Macbeth's state of mind? Explain the irony of this change.

2. List some of the specific events that Lady Macbeth refers to in her sleep-walking speeches.

3. Two place names of significance are mentioned in Scene 2. What are they, and where have you heard of them before?

4. Why is Macbeth so cocky in Scene 3? What does Macbeth's reaction to his servant tell you about him?

5. What do lines 10–16 in Scene 5 say about Macbeth's state of mind?

6. When the report comes that Birnam Wood is moving toward Dunsinane, how does Macbeth react? Why doesn't he give up right away?

7. What does Macbeth decide against in Scene 7, lines 36–38? Who is "the Roman fool" he is referring to?

8. At what point does Macbeth realize that he has been tricked?

9. In the final scene, Macbeth at one point tells Macduff, "I'll not fight with thee!" What changes his mind?

10. What does Macbeth's last line tell you about his state of mind?

11. Who will be the next king? Why? What is the mood at the end of the play?

Activities & Role-Playing **Classes or Informal Groups**

Inside Dunsinane Lady Macbeth's sleepwalking scene (Scene 1) may be one of the best-known episodes of Shakespeare's work. Read through the scene carefully. Where might it take place? Is Lady Macbeth in a room, a garden, or on a balcony? How is it lit—are there candles in holders along the walls or on

Stacy Keach as Macbeth with company in The Shakespeare Theater's 1995 production of *Macbeth* directed by Joe Dowling. Photo by Carol Rosegg.

tables? Or is there only the light from her candle? Where are the Gentlewoman and Doctor hidden? Are there night sounds—owls, dogs, or cats—or only still-ness? Present your ideas in sketches; written descriptions of the setting, light-ing, and sound effects; or a model of what the stage should look like.

War Strategy Macbeth spends most of Act 5 on an emotional roller coaster. He moves from distraction to anger, sorrow, bitterness, back to anger, and so on. How would you act this role? Working with a partner, select one scene in this act and read it aloud. Discuss how you would hold your body, move your arms, look at the other actor (or refuse to look), and walk about the stage to act out Macbeth's mood swings and reactions.

Discussion Classes or Informal Groups

1. Lady Macbeth seems like a different woman in Act 5. What has changed her? What has happened to her evil side?

2. The Witches showed Macbeth the third apparition, which stated that he would never be defeated until Birnam Wood came to Dunsinane Hill. Why then would Macbeth fortify Dunsinane instead of his former Castle Inverness?

3. Why does Macbeth treat everyone so badly? Isn't he worried about these remaining people deserting him?

4. Why would anyone still support Macbeth?

5. Why does Macbeth react the way he does to his wife's death?

6. Malcolm describes Macbeth and Lady Macbeth as "this dead butcher and his fiend-like queen." Do you agree with him?

Suggestions for Writing Improve Your Skills

1. Even though he knows he will die, Macbeth goes on fighting. Why? Pretend that you are Seton, Macbeth's aide, and that you are trying to explain Macbeth's character in a letter to a friend in England. Don't limit yourself just to Macbeth's behavior during the battle. Also include things that you learned about him as you served him from the time he was the Thane of Glamis.

2. How does Macduff feel at the end of the play? Pretend that you are Macduff and you have returned to your castle. Your wife and children are dead. Your lands were taken over while you were gone, and your servants were loyal to their new masters until the war ended. Your good friend Siward has also suffered great losses because of Macbeth. Write a letter to him describing all the things you experienced and how you feel now that it is all over.

Macbeth
Additional Resources

Books

Title: *The Riverside Shakespeare*
Author: J. J. M. Tobin et al. (editor)
Publisher: Houghton Mifflin
Year: 1997
Summary: This volume features all of Shakespeare's plays along with 40 pages of color and black-and-white plates. In addition, each play has a scholarly introduction and individual commentary. The book also contains general background material on the Shakespearean stage and Elizabethan history.

Title: *The Complete Works of Shakespeare*
Author: David Bevington (editor)
Publisher: Addison-Wesley Publishing Company
Year: 1997
Summary: This book offers the complete, unabridged works of Shakespeare as edited by the current president of the Shakespeare Association of America. Editor David Bevington also provides an introductory essay for each play and a general introduction to Shakespeare's life, times, and stage.

Title: *Shakespeare: A Life*
Author: Park Honan
Publisher: Oxford University Press
Year: 1999
Summary: Using the little available data that exists, Honan pieces together this biographical account of Shakespeare's life.

Title: *A Shakespeare Glossary*
Author: C. T. Onions (editor)
Publisher: Oxford University Press
Year: 1986
Summary: This classic reference book defines all of the now-obscure words used by Shakespeare throughout his plays. The book also uses examples and gives play locations for the words.

Title: *Shakespeare A to Z: The Essential Reference to His Plays, His Poems, His Life and Times, and More*
Author: Charles Boyce
Publisher: Facts on File
Year: 1990
Summary: This book features over 3,000 encyclopedic entries arranged alphabetically. It covers several areas of Shakespeare, including history, play synopses, and critical commentary.

Title: *The Shakespearean Stage: 1574–1642*
Author: Andrew Gurr
Publisher: Cambridge University Press
Year: 1992
Summary: Many experts consider this book to be the most authoritative text written on the theater of Shakespeare's era. This book highlights the many different theater companies of the day and how they performed.

Title: *Shakespeare's Book of Insults, Insights & Infinite Jests*
Author: John W. Seder (editor)
Publisher: Templegate
Year: 1984
Summary: This entertaining book covers several categories of jabs and mockeries taken straight from the text of Shakespeare's plays.

Title: *Everybody's Shakespeare: Reflections Chiefly on the Tragedies*
Author: Maynard Mack
Publisher: University of Nebraska Press
Year: 1994
Summary: Mack, a noted scholar, offers essays on *Romeo and Juliet, Julius Caesar, Hamlet, Othello, King Lear, Macbeth,* and *Antony and Cleopatra,* plus four chapters covering general topics. The essays are written specifically for the general reader.

Title: *The Meaning of Shakespeare* (2 vols.)
Author: Harold Goddard
Publisher: University of Chicago Press
Year: 1960
Summary: Originally published in 1951, this classic, hefty work of Shakespearean criticism includes essays on all of Shakespeare's plays. (Note: Since Goddard's work is in two volumes, readers who seek information on particular plays should make sure they obtain the volume containing commentary on that play.)

Videos

Title: *Macbeth*
Director: Philip Casson
Year: 1978
Summary: A filmed version of the play on stage: Judi Dench and Ian McKellan have the lead roles in a Royal Shakespeare Company production of the play.

Title: *Macbeth*
Director: Roman Polanski
Year: 1971
Summary: The gory action in this version represents Macbeth's descent into murderous ambition. Polanski's grisly production is notable for its impressive performances and ragged cinematography to symbolize the grim pre-Medieval Scottish setting.

Title: *Throne of Blood*
Director: Akira Kurosawa
Year: 1957
Summary: This version is one of film's greatest Shakespearean adaptations. Kurosawa masterfully transposes the play's setting from Scotland to feudal Japan. Fog, mist, and rain create an eerie visual style.

Title: *Macbeth*
Director: Orson Welles
Year: 1948
Summary: Welles creates a moody production by using sparse sets and stark lighting. Welles also gives a fine performance as the title character.

Audiotapes

Title: *Macbeth* [Abridged]
Producer: Arkangel Complete Shakespeare
Year: 1998
Summary: This audio production features a full-cast performance by members of England's professional theater community. A rousing musical score rounds out this staging.

Title: *All the World's a Stage: An Anthology of Shakespearean Speeches Performed by the World's Leading Actors*
Producer: BBC Radio
Year: 1995
Summary: A collection of some of the finest performances of Shakespeare's famous passages. Laurence Olivier, Richard Burton, and Vanessa Redgrave are featured along with several other notable actors.

Web Sites

URL: *http://www.rdg.ac.uk/globe/research/research_index.htm*
Summary: Associated with London's Globe Theatre web site, this collection of research links offers information on the building and rebuilding of The Globe, Shakespeare's relationship to the theater, and miscellaneous articles on theatrical traditions and practices during Shakespeare's time.

URL:
http://www.english.wayne.edu/~aune/2200W00Contents.html
Summary: This site offers introductory information for students studying Shakespeare. Offerings include tips for reading and writing about Shakespeare as well as information on individual works.

URL: *http://tech-two.mit.edu/Shakespeare*
Summary: This web site from the Massachusetts Institute of Technology features the full text of many of Shakespeare's plays in a searchable format.

URL: *http://shakespeare.palomar.edu//*
Summary: "Mr. William Shakespeare and the Internet" offers a wide variety of links to other Shakespeare sites. "Criticism," "Educational," and "Life & Times" are just a few of the categories offered.

Software

Title: *Macbeth*
Developer: BookWorm Student Library
Grade: 7–12, Adult
Platform: Mac, Windows
Summary: The play is presented using film, sound, graphics, unabridged original texts, and relevant criticism.

Title: *Macbeth*
Developer: Bride Digital Classic
Grade: 9–12, Adult
Platform: Windows and Mac
Summary: This software uses text, video, audio, and graphics to combine the original text with the performance of scenes.

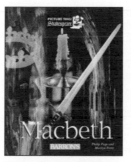

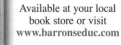

Notes

Notes